i

ISBN-10: 1070409561

ISBN-13: 9781070409566

Getting to Grace
Stories of a Bumpy Ride to Midlife

Wickham Boyle

DEDICATION

For all of us who fell down, got back up and limped toward grace.

WICKHAM BOYLE

"Some people

when they hear your

story contract.

Others upon

hearing expand

and

this is how

you

know."

Nayyirah Waheed

CONTENTS

IN THE MIRROR

"There is no greater agony than bearing an untold story inside of you."

Maya Angelou

WISDOM IN ANGER :
TO BREAK OR GLUE

Yesterday I received a package from France containing Moroccan red clay dishes that my daughter mailed me this summer from the market in Aix-en-Provence. It was six months since she purchased them and, in fact, the box had traveled far and wide — most of the dishes were broken.

I unfolded the individual plates wrapped in newspaper to see the intricate painted patterns, the lotus blossoms, the geometric shapes, concentric circles all painted in deep ocher, ebony, orange, turquoise and vibrant azure representing sea and sky. I held each dish in my hand as I assessed whether it was immediately usable, could be saved, or should be discarded.

In the middle of my dish triage I thought of a friend, a fiery Cubana, who frequents garage sales to buy crates of ugly dishes. She squirrels these ceramic disasters away in her Seattle garage and then breaks the dishes when she's in a rage. Felicia goes to her cartons and crashes the plates onto the driveway until her anger subsides. I love this idea and am jealous of her ability to own her fury and still devise a safe, cheap way to assuage her tempestuous moods.

As I sat thinking about whether I could glue the beautiful, parrot green dish back together with five-minute epoxy, carefully holding it in place until the bonding took hold, I wondered if I shouldn't maybe just smash them all on my downtown street after the kids were asleep and my husband was ensconced watching Jay Leno.

I sat on the floor debating the merits of putting something together, versus releasing its power and mine through an act of destruction. I realized I am a gluer. I hoard shards of relationships, pottery,and life and find a way to piece them back together. I held on to a relationship with the biological father of my children for decades, even after the abuse and neglect had begun to announce itself to my toddlers. I have a poem written by my daughter, then fifteen, on the occasion of my fiftieth birthday – it reads:

> "I love you because you left.
>
> Broken, but you remembered to save the pieces.
>
> Because we all glued each other back
>
> together."

It recalls the trauma when I jettisoned my nearly 20-year relationship with her father after gluing, salvaging, and wishing it would get better for far too long. Some things really should be smashed.

I am overly tenacious. I store and repair when I might be better healed by pitching, crushing, tossing, and cutting the ties. I am a believer that careful glue, and stitches in time, dinners cooked with love, and hands held can mend anything.

Now my dining room table is cluttered with broken dishes, cracked couscous bowls tipped on their sides no longer capable of holding succulent chicken, yellow broth, and floating carrots, waiting for fluffy grains of Moroccan pasta. Unlike Felicia, I can't envision myself waiting until I become angry, going to the storage closet, fetching out the correct dose of dishes needed to palliate my anger and then breaking the dishes into cosmic dust. Do I call Felicia and ask how many dishes for a broken heart, a rejected story, or an entire novel? Will Felicia respond: "Smash two cartons and call me in the morning"? And if I take these dishes down to the street, will I be arrested for disturbing the peace? Suppose someone gets a flat tire, in the February freeze, from my dish rage. Am I then responsible for changing it?

I yearn to learn when to admit defeat and toss the broken pieces in the trash. Perhaps with even more time that too will happen. But for today I have set up a workshop, and in the quiet of a late January snowstorm, I am carefully, one dish at a time, recreating the splendor that was intended by some Moroccan potter on a

Marrakech morning.

GIVE ME YOUR WORST DAYS

My 17-year-old son, Henry, just walked back into the house after a morning of "senioritis." This is a malady suffered by all high school seniors as they approach graduation; they want to do nothing and yet they desire the next phase of their life. They are bored with the tedium involved in completing high school and they yearn for the imagined fantasy awaiting them as college students living on their own. The combination of wanting to get on with their new life while attempting to wrap up the old renders them giddy and confused.

As Henry moaned and complained, "It is only Tuesday, the weekend is so far away," I decided to take a dangerous path in mothering; I chose to tell a story from my own life. Raconteurs must make sharp edits for teenagers because you have a scant window of opportunity before you are boring and they shut down. I launched into it.

I was young, in my twenties. I had finished business school and had taken a boring job working in a large foundation. The job featured humdrum employees, set hours and an over-the-top dress code. However, it paid well and offered student loan remission, two very attractive traits. So day after day I trudged from my downtown life to midtown, to the pantheon of corporate life -- the Chrysler building. Even sporting suits, nylons, silk shirts and heels, I wouldn't give up on my biking obsession. Even then I felt it defined me -- still does.

4

One Tuesday morning, yup, same day as Henry, I ran for the elevator just as the gorgeous art décor doors were about to close. There I stood, packed in with the other worker bees, and I let out a big, airy sigh. I do that often, so it comes as no surprise to my offspring that I was doing it in my 20's. Then I exclaimed, à la Henry, "Oh my God, I am so done in and it is only Tuesday!"

In the back of the elevator, wedged against the wall, was a very old man. He was dressed all in black with a large hat dangling from his right hand. The hat seemed so heavy as to pull him to that side. His head was still covered in a simple black Yarmulke. "Bad day?" he inquired, and I started to reply, but he cut me off.

"DO NOT WISH YOUR LIFE AWAY! DO NOT LOOK FOR SATURDAY ON TUESDAY! If you have bad days, any days, the worst days that you feel you can't bear to endure -- give them to me. I will take every horrible day you do not want. Give them all to me, give me your very worst days."

He spat this out and then as if some errant experimentalist directed the scene, the elevator lurched to a stop and the silver encrusted doors parted. The old man nudged his way to the front and exited.

I stood chastened. I wanted my fellow passengers to remark on the encounter, but like the motto for Las Vegas, bystanders almost never mention what happens between two New Yorkers. I rose to the 32nd floor and moped into my corner office.

I have thought about that man often. His words and their meaning were seared into my consciousness. It was as if he were a guardian angel or some pundit sent to shake my core. I hear his words whenever I want to complain about my heinous, overtaxed, scary life. I still see him wedged in the rising elevator exhorting me to send him my worst days.

It is thirty years later, and I know he is gone. He has to have passed on, even if he did find souls to share the bad days with him. He changed my life and he never knew. For him, I believe it was a gut response to a young woman who scoffed at tedium and was prone to miss the nimbus of tender light that forms a circle around us daily.

I told my son today that he should never wish part of his life away. We need to treasure all the days and not arch our vision so far forward that we miss our churning present.

NOT EVERYONE WILL LIKE YOU…
AND THAT'S A GOOD THING

Perhaps it was just being the oldest child in a family of an alcoholic father and a suicidal mother. Or my crazy, dyslexic brain that seems to reverse and skew things, giving even simple information a weird twist. But whatever it was -- nature, nurture or lack of it -- I grew into a woman who was hell-bent on pleasing people. Most of all, I wanted to win over and please those who disdained or abhorred me.

I would attempt to befriend the rabid dog, the unrideable horse, the bitchy debutante, the narcissistic man. I dated the too-handsome unavailable guys, their brothers, or my married boss. I had to be the good sport. I had to be easy because at my core, I didn't believe I had any real value other than my endless ability to put out, move furniture, and clean up messes.

I tried to win over people who did not like me or my style (too raucous, exuberant, wisecracking, occasionally phony) or who had enough friends. It didn't matter -- I had to be the most popular class mother, new worker or gym partner. If I didn't win the whole world over as active members of my fan club, I was a loser.

This was the all-too-sad truth until, mercifully, I slid into middle age. I had weathered a scandal, left an abusive relationship, won child custody battles, lost jobs, gained weight, found true love and was on a constant trek toward elevating myself and my kids to a better consciousness. In Buddhist terms, I was on a path and looking for rays of enlightenment to leak into my murky mind. One of the truths I needed to embrace was what my friend Abigail screamed at me one day through the phone.

"Everyone won't like you, you need to junk some of the ideas you have! Your ex is *never* going to say a kind word to you. The same goes for your brother and maybe some of your neighbors. If people behave as if they don't like you, back the fuck up. Do not keep going full force delivering muffin baskets to serial killers. "

OK, Abigail, I think I hear you.

And yet, there are still times when I catch myself sucking up to the rude neighbor, the woman who dismisses my every salutation until she wants help finding a parking space. I watch my mind do little gymnastic flips as it considers placing a phone call to my ex to offer a tidbit about the children's success. Then I remember the painful rebukes that only recently spewed from his mouth. Every time I call, speak to him, or send an email, the response is vitriolic and toxic. But I seem not to learn.

Banish the negative, I tell myself. Don't move toward the enemy. Now when I see someone on the street who has relayed that he or she is not among my fan base, I stop myself from hollering a big cheery hello. The deflating lack of response used to send me into a tizzy of sadness. No more of that, thank you.

Yet, I still sometimes volunteer for committees I have no interest in. I see myself smile and offer, I watch as I listen and nod when I need to run back home and write. I yearn to have the calm self-worth that allows me to say, "Margaret doesn't like me and I am fine with that." Instead, too often, there is a fantasy scenario of how I save poor Maggie from a fire, carrying her children to safety, with Wicki embraced and lauded at day's end with torrents of tears and thanks.

Get on with things, girl! You have made some egregious mistakes. You have been an occasional bitch, betrayed people, or fabricated. You did it. Oh, I could tell you about battered-woman syndrome and all the literature on children of alcoholics but no one needs more excuses or mea culpas and falls from grace.

What we need is some suck-it-up honesty. Yeah, I did wrong, I made rotten choices but I have decided to flip the script and take the high road. I still have half my life left. As my father-in-law used to say over and over, "Nothing beats a failure like a try." And so I try. Now that I am at the halfway mark, I've decided to enjoy the sensation of being accepted for who I am -- warts, scars, big heart, humor, and all. All that I am. It feels good.

STEALING HOME: FINDING FORGIVENESS

When I was 42 years old and just separated from the abusive father of my children, terrified and ensconced in a secret affair with this man's brother, I went to the home of a rich friend and stole her jewelry.

I never thought I'd be able to write that. After more than a decade, I never believed I would have the clarity, forgiveness, and inner strength to just say it. Age and time are wonderful healers.

I sat this morning watching a torrent of rain pour into my window boxes inundating the six small cypress trees I planted to give myself a sense of Christmas cheer. As I meditated, I begged my mind, my higher power, a goddess, the universe, or the watching cats, to give me the vision and gumption to write about stealing and forgiveness.

I had stolen things before. During my final years in high school my mother returned to work after a twenty-year hiatus. Our family was pretty desperate for money, as my alcoholic father's career seemed to be in a tailspin and my bipolar mom took it upon herself to save the day. She had no clothes to be a modern businesswoman (and for my mother the outfit really made the woman), so as the first child, the hero, I came to the rescue.

I went to Bloomingdale's in the mall and I shoplifted pantsuits. I then bestowed the suits on my mother. I told her I purchased them with babysitting money. I was a champion babysitter, but there weren't enough kids in Poet's Corner, our suburban neighborhood, to support these extravagant suits. My mother, as chief enabler and household master of denial, was always ready to incorporate any story, no matter how far-fetched, into her lexicon of truth. So she welcomed this wardrobe windfall and traipsed gaily off to her new job.

I continued to snag suits for her for years. Then she fell ill. She was diagnosed with Parkinson's disease and since my mother was often about appearances, she decided that her tremors were too awful for anyone to see, let alone trust her to excel in a job. She quit, and the pantsuits languished in her closet. My father retired from NBC, and they moved south to Durham, North Carolina, where he took a job running a small news station. They re-started their lives in a ranch home where my mother didn't have to climb stairs or be seen by folks she knew.

This was pretty much the end of my brilliant career as a thief. I had never thought stealing for myself was an option. Theft was something I could do for others. I didn't feel guilty about taking the outfits for my mother. I rationalized – Bloomingdale's was a conglomerate store, my mother needed this stuff, and I provided it for her. We all tell tales to justify what we do: from stealing, to sneaking the extra brownie, to having affairs. Life seemed to me to be a series of compromises regarding choices, morals, and opportunities.

Later, with my grown-up life in turmoil and my children grown to the point where they could stand up for themselves, I finally made the choice to leave their father. I decided that I couldn't take the abuse, neglect and mockery. Let's call him Dick, since it describes one of his chief characteristics. After I told Dick I was finished and he had to leave, I began an affair with his brother. My therapist said instead of just moving out of the house, I metaphorically burned it down so there would be no possibility of EVER moving back in with Dick. In a sense, having the torrid affair with Frank did inoculate me from any future relationship with Dick or his family.

I had been in an abusive relationship for almost 15 years. I am appalled to write this. I am stupefied that a strong, educated, outspoken woman put up with the kind of physical and emotional abuse I endured. I was so devalued that I came to believe I had no worth. I had fallen in love with Dick, who was handsome, aloof, under-employed, a philanderer and a full-blown narcissist. From what I had learned in my childhood, he was perfect husband material.

Dick never married me. He said he'd be damned if he would give me the opportunity to be "a fuckin' princess for a day." And yet we stayed together because a part of me felt I would never find anyone else, anyone better, and I wanted to have babies. So I called him my "husband" and got pregnant with my sweet daughter: a child whose spirit, I believed, was waiting for me to welcome her into the world. Then three years later, although Dick rarely worked, we had another baby -- a boy. My fantasy family was complete. I had what my mother called "The choice of kings -- *le choix des rois*," a boy and a girl. I also had a man who cheated, belittled me, spat at me, shoved me and tossed me down a flight of stairs while I was pregnant. Dick always said, "I never hit you." Moral hair-splitting. Since I produced theater for a living, I continued spinning illusions with my personal life. I worked endless hours, pretended everything was fine, yet I was miserable and terrified. I had no idea where to turn. After creating this elaborate fantasy I couldn't admit to any of my friends how degraded I was.

Dick and I were in therapy where he disclosed how his father had sexually molested two of his sisters and this fact illuminated the roots of his emotional withholding. I was convinced I could "save" him, since this was my childhood role. However, neither of us transcended our broken beginnings. I was always the angry, disappointed mother and he was an angry, fuck-up father. We made a perfect pact of complicit insanity. We stayed locked in this baleful world where I begged for attention, affection, sex, financial assistance, any bone he would toss me, and he gleefully withheld and played the uptown gigolo. It was pathetic.

It was my daughter, then eight-years-old, who came to my rescue. One early morning, as I was picking up clothes, washing dishes, calling my assistant, and getting kids ready for school while the man of the house slept in the big feather bed, my angel whispered, "Mama, when you are the woman, does it mean that you do all the work, earn all the money, and pick up after everyone and the man yells at you? And why do the kids have to pick up clothes if Papa doesn't have to do anything?"

The circuit in my badly wired brain flipped, as if my internal sanity signal, which had been stuck in the off position for decades, switched on. This farce of a relationship would stop. I was done. I began to formulate an exit strategy. Even if I couldn't take care of myself, I was not going to doom my children to a life where they learned abuse.

I canceled our family summer vacation, the one where I would pay for everything and Dick would complain and berate me. Instead I took the kids away to visit friends in the south of France. Before leaving, I sat down with Dick at our kitchen table and told him I was finished. I wrote out my speech on a scrap of paper. I had scribbled it over and over in my journal trying to find the essence of why I could no longer go on. Imagine, I felt compelled to find the right words to express why I was leaving a man who had never supported our family and had been stone cold mean to me for years. Dick told me I was totally negative and there was nothing redeeming about me. I told him I couldn't listen to those characterizations any more. I further, and perhaps in a foolhardy way, told him I believed in magic and a sense the world was wonderful and there was a gentle universe waiting to connect me to other like-minded spirits. Dick scoffed and rejected any notion of magic. He thought I was a lunatic.

Dick didn't object, or even negotiate staying. He moved out ahead of schedule on July 4th right before I went on vacation with the kids. I was 42 years old and about to have a real Independence Day. As we formulated his exit strategy, we fell into a bitter fight. Dick ran after me trying to beat me with a set of crutches he was using for a severed Achilles tendon and I threatened police action. When he left the house it was cold and final.

As much as I wanted to believe in magic, I was so broken I imagined no one would ever love me again. I would be that lone woman in the diner with no partner, no sweetheart. I felt my sexuality had been so degraded by the years spent with Dick's affairs and insults including calling me a fat pig -- I sought to restart my erotic engine by having an affair with his brother Frank.

Frank and I had always been drawn to each other; we both had a raucous sense of humor, we had very judgmental spouses who disdained us and castigated us, often in public. The affair was wrong. I know that. Frank had a wife and two little kids, but I knew he had been having affairs for his entire marriage and in my neediness I rationalized that I needed him and the rest be damned.

It was the same sensation when I stole the jewels at a friend's Thanksgiving breakfast. They were there on the bathroom counter, and in a drawer. I put my hand out, filled my purse and left with my kids. I believed this stolen jewelry could save my children, save me, and even -- this is so stupid -- save my neighbor across the street who was in the process of attempting to leave her abusive husband. I rationalized that I was Robin Hood.

The universe and my destiny had a different scenario in mind. After the theft, I called a society woman, who I assumed was a friend, and asked her how I could sell some jewelry in order to raise funds to finalize my separation from Dick. She invited me to her Upper East Side home and had a sting set up. The family from whom I had stolen surmised I had done it and must have contacted a variety of people, putting out the word. When I arrived uptown there was a former prosecutor and the husband of the woman from whom I had stolen the jewels. I was caught. It was mind-boggling. I kept saying, *Please don't take my kids from me. Please, I am so desperate, please don't take my kids. I will do anything you ask.* That's all I can remember, except that I felt as if there was no air. And that outside it was raining and cold, just like it is today.

I have to stop.

Ten years have passed and still I can't escape the sickness in my muscles as I write this -- the shame, the terror, the horrible notion that I blew up my life and hurt others. I risked my children's future all because I believed I had so little value, so little hope, that I had to steal.

My life began to go into free fall as I was sucked into a vortex. I can see now, in retrospect, that this explosion set me on the course to find my real path, but in the middle of the crash the dust and debris were daunting. The woman who conducted the sting, Trixie, called my ex. She also called many of the benefactors for my non-profit theater and she called the press. She did this even though the people from whom I had stolen signed a pact specifying no one involved would talk about this, ever. I agreed to seek professional counseling and we would all move on with our lives. It was incredibly generous on their part, but Trixie had other plans.

Within weeks, right before Christmas, a tabloid paper ran the story of my thievery featuring Trixie as the savior. My affair with Frank was there, as was my separation from Dick, who it turned out had been having affairs with many society women. He was pictured as a poor, beleaguered patsy. I was conjured as some sort of seasoned thief with a nefarious mind and a lair into which I could slink.

I saw my life evaporate. I panicked. I could not see my way out. I was going to be a waitress in a fast food restaurant. Okay, I could do that. I would move, start again and build a tiny, clean, untainted life for my little family and myself. The press was calling my house, and then my ex would call to gloat and threaten to take the children away from me forever. He chanted into the phone, "I will *destroy* you!" Dick had found a way to continue his abuse, but it was I who handed him the tools.

I took Nyquil every night after I put the kids to bed and cried myself to sleep. I awoke in the morning groggy with sopping wet pillows. I made strong black coffee, forced a smile and got back on the path. I was psychotic every time the children had to visit Dick for a weekend. I convinced myself I would never see them again. All the grants for my theater dried up and I considered killing myself, but I couldn't possibly leave my darling children with Dick.

I called my best girlfriend, my heart, and my partner in the little theater I began downtown after leaving La MaMa. Kass also worked as a concierge in a fancy uptown hotel. This was the first time I had admitted my culpability to anyone other than the prosecutor involved in the sting. To the outside world I attempted to brush this off as gossip initiated by a vengeful ex. Like a child afraid of bad dreams, I felt if I kept denying that any of it was true, it would go away. Kass was on duty at the front desk and as she checked in Prince, she simultaneously read me the riot act.

"Under no circumstances are you to consider killing yourself. You are not your mother. You are too strong for that. You must never let Dick win. You stole stuff; that's bad, but there are no charges. You will rebuild your life better than before. Believe me. We will make this work. You have to go through fire now. You were a piece of pottery and the fire is at your heels. You have the opportunity to become porcelain if you make it through without cracking. I have confidence in you and *fuck* the rest of them. I will call you back."

Kass hung up the phone and I sat for hours in the same chair, frozen in place. She called back, and we planned to shut down our theater in the New Year and to put one foot in front of the other.

The stories in the newspapers didn't stop for five years. Every time I got a job there would be another story and it would be sent to my boss. I changed careers, moving into the financial services sector where an FBI background check was conducted and where prospective stockbrokers have to pass rigorous qualifying exams. I passed and was building a business, but still the hounding continued. I began to look for jobs with my bad press clippings in hand, and I even landed some, but then Trixie or Dick would call and harass the bosses until I was fired. I felt mired in shame and terror.

When I lived with Dick I felt unsafe because of the battering and assaults, but even with Dick out of my home he continued to pursue me. Dick sued to take the children away even though he had no apartment and no job. By the time the hearing came I was vice president in a brokerage firm, living in the children's original home; as Dick's accusations were not substantiated, the court awarded me full custody. But his abuse did not abate. It was up to me to find my own safety in the midst of the continued onslaught.

I cried, I smashed things, I cooked and cleaned, and I called my friends, who counseled me to believe this crisis was all part of a plan and promised life would improve. They prescribed forward motion, continued therapy, and forgiveness. The last part has been the most difficult, because too often what I wanted was revenge.

I enrolled in a small Buddhist school where I learned meditation and yoga. I was introduced to the teachings of the Dalai Lama who preaches that we all need to offer forgiveness to those who have hurt us most and accept their venom back as a neutralizing process. I wrote letters of amends to some I had harmed. I tried to get up every morning and do good work, help people, be kind and believe in action as a great healer. I had good moments and very low moments.

I fell in love with a wonderful man named Zachary. I told him everything. Emblematic of his spirit, after I disgorged the story of my theft, he took me by the hand to the Metropolitan Museum on Fifth Avenue and in the Temple of Dendur he said with firm rectitude, "Look at all this shit. All of it was stolen." We left; enough said. He loved me, proposed later in the year and we got married. My husband adored me and supported me when I was fired and broken. He encouraged me to be a writer, which had always been my heart's desire. He said, "Baby, you need to know. When the phone rings asking to complain to the boss, you can respond, she's right here." Rather than fire myself, I needed to forgive.

I struggled, I worked, I volunteered, I mothered, I laughed outrageously as I strove to forgive myself for the abuse I welcomed and for the lack of faith I evinced in my own abilities. I began to admit that I had not lived an exemplary life. I had been mean, less than generous, manipulative. I could do better. I tried to forgive myself for resorting to thievery rather than believing that there was help available. I focused on forgiving myself while I reveled in writing, the work I always wanted. I now regard the past decade with a wide-eyed sense of wonder.

I left a relationship where I was abhorred, where I worked in jobs that gave me low remuneration and terrible esteem. I rebuilt my life out of the rubble. I fell in love with a man who refused to judge me, who was present and supportive of my every transformation. I have used my transgressions as a teaching tool, a parable reminding my kids that there is nothing from which we can't recover. I have told them everything. I remind them that since I made this big misstep and have been honest with them about it, then perhaps it creates an atmosphere where they will believe that there is nothing they can do that will appall me. I will listen. We will learn and do better.

In the rubble of my life I found good building materials for forgiveness. What facilitates forgiveness still stymies me. Perhaps it is the cessation of rushing hormones flanked by the simple passage of time, or the realization that holding hate is a great toxin, one I am free to release. I may not have become the precious porcelain my girlfriend predicted, but I am on a path. I fell down and broke, but I remembered to take all the pieces, and with love, with friends, and with forgiveness I am piecing it together.

RING THE BELL

After I stole the jewelry, I was touted in the press as a consummate thief, a person who didn't work, but rather stole things to support whatever my supposed habits were. I could no longer keep my non-profit theater going. Who was going to give a grant to such a nefarious character? I had to close it, let all the employees go, and get on with my life, which included supporting two small children.

There was no child support, my supposed "friends" shunned me, the real friends in my life stayed close and we tried to work it out, but I was sinking into even deeper despair. What could be more profound than stealing to support your kids?

I needed work. One of my close single mom friends was having an affair with a principal in a Wall Street firm and she sent me to him. I said, "I am 44 years old, I have an MBA from Yale, and two kids to feed. I think I can be a stockbroker. My father told me I could sell refrigerators to Eskimos. Give me a chance." I did not tell him, "I am embroiled in a scandal where my ex will hound me wherever I go and by the way, I *did* steal the jewels from the nice people uptown. But, hey listen - I gave them back."

I met with my friend's paramour, a six-foot, six-inch man whose body appeared to have melted in the center, giving him the demeanor of Humpty Dumpty in a bespoke suit. But hell, Meg thought he was hot, so I flirted, projected bright and confident, and flashed my MBA. He hired me on my 44th birthday. I splurged on a half-bottle of Château d'Yquem, some paté and green salad, and rode my bike home to celebrate with my fiancé. I would be paid $500 a week to be an apprentice stockbroker. I had to take a hellish six-hour exam and have an FBI background investigation, but today, I was on a path. A middle aged woman radically changing careers and full of hope.

I started on the following Monday. I rode uptown to the boutique brokerage firm dubbed "Firestarter" by the rookie brokers. The brokerage firm was comprised mostly of young men and there was a rhythm and lingo like a fraternity. Brokers were separated into groups called "pods," like whales. This was, I presume, to encourage us to believe that we should be looking only for big fish to catch as clients. Everything was geared to reminding you to find only the cream of the crop— *do* more, *make* more. This translated into *being* more.

Each pod had a mentor. Mine was Roberto Gallo, *Bob*. Bob Gallo reminded me, at least for his elegance and Americanization, of my maternal grandfather. Pasquale Giuseppe Piccirilli hailed from Carrara, Italy, the region known for flawless marble. He descended from a family of sculptors and artists, but in America, when he attended Columbia School of Engineering and later in the Navy, he was *P.J.* or *Pic*. Gallo took the same route, swapping the music for the blunt sounds in American male names.

Bob was a small, trim, fit man -- impeccable to the point of obsession. And even though most of the other rookie brokers towered over him, Bob ruled supreme, the biggest fish in the pond. My three other pod mates were: Chip, a literal giant retired from the Italian basketball league; Len, a long drink of working class water from the east end of Long Island; and Fritz, a fat high school dropout who was a whiz in math, but otherwise nearly pre-verbal. We sat at desks that surrounded Bob, and we listened and cold-called clients in an attempt to qualify them to speak with our boss. Cold calling, before regulations countermanded it, was the main method used by many firms of finding new clients. You called from new lists presented every day, and attempted to get the folks who answered to talk to you long enough to interest them in what you had for sale. It could be vacuum cleaners, snake oil or in this case, stocks.

I actually loved doing this. Of course it was perfect for me: talking people who had no connection to me into liking me. I had done this all my life and, in fact, the more hostile, the bigger and better the challenge. I refused to work from the script that we were given. I made conversation. If potential clients asked for "quotes," that meant they wanted us to look up where a certain stock was trading. This was just before the Internet hit big and people still needed brokers. Instead of giving the price, I'd quote Shakespeare, "Tomorrow and tomorrow creeps in this petty pace from day to day… Oh, wait – did you want another quote? Chrysler: 35 and five eighths." Before stocks were finally converted into decimals, they ran in obscure fractions, so I had to have a conversion chart in front of me so I could know if 5/8 was more or less than ⅓. Alternately, I had to holler at Fritz.

I became known as the quoting broker and some of Bob's clients would ask for me by name. Others would say, "Give me the broker who gives you the quote before she gives you the quotes." I had success with clients. After all, I was twenty years older than the other whales-in-training and I had some business background. I also knew that I wanted to be scrupulously honest. I had trod that other path. It was too tempting and I needed to be vigilant. I was.

I biked to work early, changed my clothes in the elevator, cold called, drank tons of coffee and began to open accounts for Bob. One day I was adjusting my skirt and buttoning my blouse as I stepped out into the 52nd floor and the receptionist said to me. "Do you know we have a video feed from the elevator to this desk?" *Oops.* Dora told me that some of the guys get here early to watch me change, "The boss likes it cause he hadn't been able to entice them into coming to work before the bell rings, and now they gather round my desk, watchin' you transform from bike messenger to broker." Mind you, I was never even in skivvies; I just buttoned up, hid my parka and sweat pants and fluffed up a bit, but later I found a coffee shop restroom in the lobby and arrived ready to roll before I hit the elevator. They had to pay me more if I was going to be motivational material.

I worked. I studied at breaks for the licensing exam, called *Series 7* and *63*. I had passed my FBI investigation; hence, I knew that all the charges, harangues and terror were only complaints and no legal action had been taken. I could begin to work in an arena where decisions were not made on rumor and reputation. I studied harder. I still had the kids, my sweet lover and the gut-wrenching fear generated by my ex, Dick, regarding my misdeeds and how he intended to hound me with them.

Dick called at work threatening me, scaring me and reducing me to tears. It wasn't enough that he contributed nothing to raising the kids; he was also disrupting my meager ability to care for them. My wonderful gay, Buddhist assistant tried to make light of my ex's calls at work by announcing, "Mr. Richard Breath is on line one." Even though I appreciated his pluck, I was terrified.

My weeping was a distraction. Bob Gallo took me to lunch. We went to a small Italian restaurant. If the *Sopranos* had existed I would have believed we were on the set. Bob ordered the house wine, he flirted with the waitress, a woman who he confided was one of his "goombahs" (his lovers). He had five kids and a wife in Jersey, but he had to practice his craft, and for that, a man needed an outside professional. He said all of this with such aplomb, that I began to buy it. Gallo was the consummate broker and he was selling *me*.

I relaxed. He took my hands across the table. My heart flipped into my gut. Yuck. But he didn't hit on me. Instead he said. "Your ex, he calls, he threatens you, and he distracts you. You have two beautiful children and a good man who loves you. What is the matter?"

I broke down. I told him about the abuse, about my stealing. He stopped me. His voice became a stage whisper, "Stop. Do not cheapen yourself with this. When you are ready, I will make all of this go away. But you must be ready. You must know beyond doubt when you come to me. When you come to me to ring the bell . . . you must know that bell cannot be unrung." And then he continued, "That is what people forget. I have spoken to you about buyer's remorse with clients -- this is the same thing. Come to me. Say, 'Roberto, I want to ring the bell'. Then walk away from me and you will never again get another phone call from that asshole to make you cry. He is less than a man, and I do not believe in knees or limping. It is only rung or un-rung for me. I have no interest in the middle. Now eat."

I stopped crying. After all, I was in a mafia film and the pasta was getting cold, so I ate and we went back to work. I told no one about this talk for months. And the phone kept ringing and I cried in the bathroom or sniffled at my desk. Every day the bell rang to launch the opening of the market and Bob would glance at me and say, "This day has begun, and the bell has rung. Start to work and remember."

After Dick called during dinner one night and told my fiancé that he was, "a slave, and that was why he could stay with me and take care of his children." I saw my proud, strong, African American husband put his head on the table and cry. The kids hugged him and we recomposed our little family, but now I wanted to share what Gallo had offered.

I told Zach replete with *sotto voce* intonations and hand gestures. It wasn't funny yet. We actually discussed it and came to the conclusion that there were a number of moral obstacles to this course of action. As silly as it sounds, there was Karma, or as Zach parsed it, "what goes around, comes around." And there was the notion that taking Dick out of the picture might turn him into a martyr. Zach counseled letting Dick live his life and we would continue to step up and try to live ours.

Yet, during the financial news, when the bell rings heralding the start or end of another day on Wall Street, I couldn't help but think.

SELLING HOME

For 38 years, I lived in a loft at 38 North Moore Street, in what became chic TriBeCa. When I moved there it wasn't such a difficult word to type. We called it "downtown" or "Washington Market," the term the butter and egg guys used for the area. It became the **TRI**angle **BE**low **CA**nal Street after a few years when artists colonized the cavernous spaces. We didn't care that there were no services.

I rode my bike everywhere and returning home from my work at the experimental theater La MaMa, I would watch the bodegas disappear, the Italian markets vanish, and it became ghostly quiet as I clattered over cobblestones below Canal. I knew I was approaching my destination when the treasured childhood aroma of hay and horses wafted out from the Police stable as I zoomed by. Home.

Home is difficult to sell as it is a concatenation of experiences: first love, divorce, September 11th, boy and girl babies coming home, then leaving for dances, college and returning for heartbreak and joy. Our space was huge, a big barn furnished with every cumbersome piece of furniture friends wanted to unload and oodles of donated art from people like De Kooning and Fischl, as well as children's doodles. The loft had collected tribal art and artifacts from my childhood travel and then stops I made working in international theater and as a travel writer. My friends call the loft "The Museum of Wicki" and I adored it.

But I couldn't afford to live in TriBeCa any more. I had taken a Home Equity loan, HELOC, against the value of my loft and for ten years I utilized it to pay for Columbia and

Skidmore, buy a place in the country and cover the lean times ubiquitous to a family of consultants and students. When I realized that my loan would flip from interest only at a low rate, to paying off the principal as well, I knew we had to leave.

In October 2015 we had an all-building owners' meeting and I came back to our loft firm in my resolve to sell. The maintenance was rising, the mix of owners had flipped from an artist mentality to a maximize and monetize mentality and we needed to march on.

I always thought I would sell the loft myself. Why not? I had run and launched a number of businesses and I had an MBA from a school in New Haven, and this gave me some biz bravery. But then the world started to scare me. Suppose I blew it? This was my, our, only retirement fund. I'd never gotten a pension, I had a small IRA and I had been wise about real estate, but as I learned in B School, cash is king and I had very little of that. Would a broker make me more money that the 6% I would pay her, and would it make the experience more felicitous?

First, I found a lawyer. A wonderful, left leaning, silver haired woman a stone's throw from the loft downtown. I loved her. I trusted her. She charged a flat fee, not drumming up hours by making legal mischief. We were a team.

Then, I interviewed a few brokers. All nice, a little scary, some pushy, and most didn't understand what I was selling. They wanted me to paint, to stage the place; basically tart it up. So instead I wrote this ad and asked a colleague who ran the online magazine, TriBeCa Citizen, if he'd post it as a lark.

"Hidden Treasure in TriBeCa: 2200 sq. feet, a beauty from 1897, on the epicenter block of chic TriBeCa is yours to purchase and transform. Why settle for someone else's architectural vision when you can create your own? Long time

TriBeCa artist residents selling their Cond-Op loft. Perfect rambling space, large north facing windows, and some south as well, designated roof space for central air. Live like an artist now, or take down to bones and create your own magic. Great schools, restaurants, access to parks, the river and subways. $2.7 million"

The editor, with whom I had worked at Budget Travel, made some tweaks and suggested that interested parties reply to the magazine and then he would send them on to me. Nice intrigue.

And folks came. Lovely people, families, movie stars, and one broker. The broker entered and stammered, "Oh this will never do."

I asked her to give me her phone.

"Why?"

"I want to call your mother and see who raised you. This is my home. Leave now."

"Well, I might have people who could be interested."

"Oh no, you are in the penalty box. Leave!"

And she took her four-inch heels and clickety-clacked out the door. A houseguest from Italy emerged from the guest bedroom and said, "Was there just a cold wind that came through?" And we doubled over in laughter.

I would never have been able to banish someone if a broker had been involved. I would have kowtowed to her image of who should live in my beloved home. But instead I waited for a full six days, until an acquaintance sent the buyers our way.

I loved them immediately. Both were video game designers in their early 40's and newly married. They were sweet, open hearted and excited by our home and making it theirs. When they came back for a second look they asked if I would adjust the price downward as the building carries some debt.

"Who told you about the debt?"

"Well, you did."

"Yes, because I want a totally transparent deal where we talk to each other and make it simple. So no, I already took into account the debt when I made a fair price."

The man stood up and walked across my big front room with his hand out. I shook it and began to weep. His wife, my husband and our friend all came and hugged me. I am told it is an unusual end to a real estate deal. That was November 1, 2015. Real Estate deals, at least in New York City, have a semi-glacial pace. The prospective buyer and I instituted a weekly email check-in. Every Monday we wrote an email saying what was transpiring in the deal, and exchanged chit chat. We signed a contract the day before Thanksgiving, meaning ten percent of the sale price goes into escrow. Then it seemed like an eternity, until early March, before the co-op board agreed to meet the prospective buyers. This wonderful, fiscally sound couple charmed them.

March was torture: we rented a wonderful, light-filled apartment in Harlem and began moving up there little by little. But I was terrified that the loft deal wouldn't go through. The co-op had some issues. The closing date appeared and then was canceled. I feared we would be stuck with two places and no capital to run them. I had gone out on a big limb and terror began to set in. I wasn't sleeping, I was fretting about everything and driving my family crazy. The co-op was being hateful, which had the wonderful effect of banishing any nostalgia about leaving home. We finally closed on April 1, exactly 38 years to the day of when I moved into the loft boasting an 8-foot couch, a trapeze and a plastic shower. Now it took two trucks to cart stuff uptown or to the barn in the country.

Gone were the days of tossing keys wrapped in mismatched socks out the window to let in visitors, since there was no intercom. The freight elevator was now stainless steel. Everything under the sun could be delivered to your downtown door and taxis certainly knew where North Moore Street was. I thought I would be like Lyubov Ranevskaya in *The Cherry Orchard*, running throughout my place touching the walls extolling my beautiful Thanksgiving dinners for 40, or the myriad benefits we hosted, the sleepovers, the guests from far and near, the pole marking the height of everyone who wandered in and the progress of tall children, or the Halloween parties where dry ice made smoke ooze from under the bathroom door. But there was no melancholy. I was ready to leave. Cleaning, packing, carting, hauling, tossing, that was hard. But leaving TriBeCa, selling my home, that was the correct choice.

Now where did I put my bike keys? I want to explore my new neighborhood.

ME TOO, ALSO

The table in my Harlem nest was set for two -- candles, flowers and bottles of wine lined up like happy gymnasts awaiting a turn at the balance beam. My longtime, great, wise friend was coming to dinner. It was supposed to be dinner for four, but wonderfully, schedules conspired to bring two old friends together for hours of uninterrupted conversation.

There was never a need to question the long circular conversations about producing experimental theater (we both did it), or to apologize to others for a sidebar on an arcane tidbit regarding dance companies in Laos or boutique hotels in Paris. We understood each other inside and out. We had weathered various partners, job changes and geographic separations, but we always came together over theater and great food.

I say we are the same vintage. To me that means we share a terroir and a provenance. We may not be exactly the same age, but close enough to share all the musical, political and sartorial touchstones. There is a shorthand and an ability to listen to long stories, nod or leap in with a thought. Our time together is a thorough joy.

At our dinner, I inadvertently brought up the horrible orange monster masquerading as president, and my friend put up his long, elegant hand, "I don't talk about him. And if asked when I am oversees, I demur saying, I am not an American; I am a New Yorker." Funny, I said that many times when Bush II was president. Sadly, upon reflection, those look like halcyon days. And so we backed away from that minefield and talked about our colleagues and my friend's future direction after his long anticipated retirement.

We careened to the *Me Too* movement after a discussion of the conductors, choreographers and theater artists among those indicted. We trod paths of our careers working with artistic directors we knew to be brutal, abusive and downright difficult. Yet the difficult people with whom we worked had not crossed the boundary to sexual abuse. In conversation, lubricated by copious red wine, I dipped a toe into a question I had been struggling with since *Me Too* tales began rolling out like waves across the news and social media. It became a tsunami for me; I felt every new revelation because it seemed to tear off the carefully placed Band-aids and scabs I had cultivated. And then the shame and uncertainty surrounding how and when I had been complicit settled on me. It was thick.

I relived every time I didn't push back with foundation executives where I wanted the grant, even when the aged hands got handsy. I was newly taunted by my giggles and glee at the stupid remarks I treated as glorious wisdom. I recalled accepting a car ride home from rehearsal only to have the production manager actually stick his tongue down my throat when we reached my West Village apartment. My horror was compounded when my then boyfriend laughed at this old man coming on to me. And as this former sweetie is still a friend, I was revolted when he recently said "Remember when PL slipped you the tongue?" Of course, I remember. I still can't drive or bike by the Upper East Side church where we were rehearsing without feeling nauseous. I had to continue working with him after the incident and be chipper and bright and none-the-worse-for-wear. I squirm in my seat experiencing a physical malaise at the recall of being chased around a desk at a prestigious midtown magazine by an old scion of literature. He had met me at a party at Gracie Mansion and asked me my aspirations. I sent him some written work. He invited me to his tower to talk. I thought he was taken with my prowess as a cunning linguist. Rather, I discovered he had a trail of very young, curvy, Irish-y girls who had been sucked in with the same pitch. Some stayed and were promoted, others fled into the night to ride their bikes home crying, feeling stupid, unworldly and definitely not a good writer. No one would treat a fine writer that way. Right?

Our dinner conversation veered to his admission that he had never been stalked in that manner. "I wasn't a pretty young boy," he shared in a matter-of-fact way. But he said he had heard legions of stories for decades about young boys of color plucked from choruses and orchestras and neither he nor anyone else had done anything until now. I wondered if since the entitled men who had abused my trust and body were no longer alive, was I then obviated from the necessity of coming out against them? Do we all have to come forward with more vital actions than just clicking social media boxes, signing petitions and sighing in relief when it gets a tad better?

The subtle and not-so-subtle ways in which vulnerable people, men and women, girls and boys are subjugated is terrifying. In my day and in my mother's day it was unconscious acquiescence, unless you were forcibly raped. Whatever else you did to lubricate the wheels of your life, your career, your theater was accepted. Heck, it was largely expected. And I am ashamed of it.

If the men who took advantage of my need for work or funding were still alive, would they feel shame, or remorse? I doubt it. I believe that there was a level of -- call it complicity or acting that we or I perfected so they would not feel uncomfortable, creepy or craven. That is another part of what I feel so undone by. When I was with men of my own status, if I was interested, I indulged; if not, I got out of there. I never wanted to slap a face and say, "UGH, you are disgusting," however, that is what I should have said to

Handsy and Tongue Monster and their ilk But I was silent, and instead, poured on the charm. Does this make me responsible for when they did it again and again? Because they are no longer orbiting in this realm and there is no alarm to sound to protect others, what is my responsibility and my resolution? I imagine like most difficult things, the crux of the matter lies deep within me. I have to forgive myself first for my infractions, real and magnified over decades. I knew better. I complied sometimes and at other moments I took that bike and rode home.

EASY DOES IT

Don't cry because it's over, smile because it happened.

\-   *Dr. Seuss*

DIVINE WISDOM OF THE ABSURD

Being adored for blue eyes, apple pies, my ability to ride a wild pony, dissect a spreadsheet, comfort a caterwauling child, and whip up a dinner while wearing lacy panties all in the same day—if not in the same hour—no longer seems so important as my life elongates and I find myself in my middle years. It occurs to me I've spent too much time racing to the next place in my mind; making love but thinking about what time the kids come home; helping with homework and making a stock trade; finishing one task and making the next list, rushing through everything, trying to be perfect.

I've begun to wonder why being able to do everything, and do it well, was once in my view, an attribute of perfection.

At this age, all I've done, all that business is a blur compared to the few brief mad moments when I've forgotten myself, forgotten what I meant to do, look like, and act like. The rare instances when I've gone beyond the heartbreaking judgments of others, when I've had glimpses of how beautiful and desirable life really is, have had nothing to do with doing everything. In fact my experience of true freedom has been in bursts of divine absurdity.

My own tale of exalted freedom took place on a fall day about 20 years ago when the sky was scrubbed blue and the air was crisp enough to bite back, but not leave marks.

I was a young mother, working full-time as the executive director of the experimental theater group La MaMa, located in New York City's bohemian East Village. La MaMa was one of the first off-center theater companies that began in the very experimental '60s. Even after 50 plus years La MaMa is still in the forefront of the *avant-garde* and was continuously led by its founder, the charismatic, irrepressible and feisty octogenarian Ellen Stewart. In 1969 Ms. Stewart had the prescience to cobble together a group of playwrights, actors, designers and composers from many different parts of the world, creating a sense of global, multi-disciplinary dramatic fusion. They launched a genre of theater in which anything was possible.

La MaMa (Ellen was "mama" to all the actors who came through her doors, "La" was a nod to her Cajun roots) was my first job after I graduated from New York University. I was enthralled with the electricity there and knew I was around something incredible. I wanted to be useful, and vital too. I wasn't an actor – I was a techie.

Everyone did everything. We had to; there was so little money and so much to do, but it was thrilling. I met Harvey Fierstein, the famous drag queen, before his roles in *Mrs. Doubtfire* and *Hair Spray* (I remember bumping into this "woman" on the backstairs at the theater who growled, "Well, excuse you"). Playwright/actor Sam Shepard, Bette Midler, Diane Lane, Robert De Niro, Harvey Keitel, and Billy Crystal—we literally grew up together at that theater. We were all united by La MaMa.

After working for a while as a techie and stage manager, I went back to school and garnered an MBA from Yale. I returned to La MaMa to take on the role of Executive Director. I need to be clear: this was not a job description. That would read: "The Executive Director is responsible for any extraneous thing that can go wrong in producing 60 shows each season – fundraising, marketing, contracts, and artistic soothing. Please note many productions will be with companies from outside the United States and there will be endless visa, grant, attitude problems and communication gaps." The job description would further read, "If anything goes wrong, it is the fault of the Executive Director, however if success ensues, someone else will get kudos."

Well, this was the job for me: all the work, none of the glory. We all sacrificed because we believed in something – that theater was a balm for the soul. And on nights when the lights dimmed and, for example, a production of *Antigone*, all done in Native American Yup'ik, made the audience shake the rafters with applause, I knew that my commitment was not misplaced. At the core of my job description was the mandate that I raise enough money in grants from foundations, corporations, and the government so that the work of hundreds of artists could continue. I took the job seriously. I felt as if the entire operation relied on me. I felt this so deeply that after I had given birth to my daughter on a Saturday night, after having worked Friday and gone into labor at the theater, I returned to work on Tuesday, taking my newborn daughter, Sarah Wilson, called "Willi," with me on my bicycle.

My wonderful midwife told me there was no endeavor that couldn't be continued if the mom had mastered it before becoming pregnant. So I had ridden my bike every day while pregnant and ridden by bike home from La MaMa in labor.

As a theater baby, Willi was a constant presence at rehearsals of all sorts: Greek classics, *Medea*, *The Trojan Women*, *Electra* and *Oedipus*, all performed with liberal poetic license. Plays might be chanted in ancient Greek, lit with oil torches or performed in modern dress with all-female casts – nothing was off limits. Actors, including the guys from the Blue Man Group or John Leguizamo, would stop by the office on the top floor of the old sausage-factory-cum-theater and ask me if they could take the baby to rehearsal or on their lunch break. They knew I rarely had a babysitter and many of them had grown up in big families and understood the kind of volunteerism necessary to make a not-for-profit theater function. I had known many of these actors, carpenters, and jack-of-all-trade theater folks for more than a decade. I had been on tours across Europe or up all night preparing productions with them. This was my extended family. But it had a difficult matriarch. Ellen Stewart was the queen; I was always trying to please her and I never quite felt my efforts were satisfactory.

On this particular autumn day, I had been slaving over a major grant application to the National Endowment for the Arts. If we received this grant, it would support our entire next season. For me to write this, I needed a certain mindset. No distractions – not hair in my face nor growling stomach, telephones ringing nor crying baby. I had eaten, sent my toddler off to a rehearsal with a company of whirling dervishes visiting from Turkey, and I shut off the phone. But I was still distracted by my hair. I have always had a mane of thick Italian tresses, with a life of their own, and I found I was spending far too much time brushing it aside or attempting to smooth it down. I could not locate a rubber band or anything to tie back my hair. In desperation to get on with my work, I took a pair of cotton toddler training panties out of the baby bag and pulled them on my head. I tugged the hair out of the little leg holes in two tufts and, finally, I was able to concentrate. I settled in to write.

I wrote the grant all day. I was productive and felt content by late afternoon when it was time to ride my bike home. I retrieved Willi, who was now being fed sticky rice by the Japanese carpenters, perched her in the backpack into which, by now, she just barely fit, and off we went home on my green Raleigh three-speed. Willi loved the breeze and the world whizzing by.

I loved the freedom, the exercise and the thriftiness of a

bike. On the bike, I never had to rely on anyone else. The bus may be late, the subway inexplicably stops and cash flow makes cabs off limits; so my bike became my gym, my transportation, and a boost for my spirits.

I proceeded across East 4th Street to the Bowery, flowing with traffic through the East Village. I enjoyed my time on the bike – it was private and provided me with plenty of thinking space. That day my head was full of ideas for the proposal and I was in love with the world. I was a mother who could be with her baby and have a full time job. I made my own hours, my kid made my day, and I was on my bike pedaling toward home in slanted late fall sunshine.

I was high on life and it was one of those moments when I could see it translating to everyone. The world smiled at me. I was a wonder. They could see that I was successful and maybe even a little sexy with my thick thighs pushing along. I felt as if I had a brilliant mind and exuded a positive spirit flowing from doing good work. The waves and grins of greeting continued as I glided west to go shopping for dinner. The grocer was packed, and there was a long line snaking to the cashier. I clutched my basket of food and chatted to my girl on my back. The crowd parted before me saying, "Please, why don't you go first, you have the baby." Everyone was smiling. I beamed. I was beatific.

In the bakery, I was again showered with grins and speedy service. The same happened in the deli. Then I packed my bundles into the newsboy basket on the front of my bike and pedaled down Seventh Avenue toward home. People in cars waved and I felt deliriously happy and smug. "You see, great moods really are contagious," I said to Willi as I smiled and waved back at my admirers.

Once home, I hauled the groceries and my girl up four flights of stairs. Even this felt great – *see, I could* do it all! I went into the bathroom to wash my hands and happened to glance in the mirror. "Oh my God," I said out loud: "I HAVE UNDERPANTS ON MY HEAD!"

I marched to the phone and called the theater in an outrage—how could they let me leave with children's underpants on my head? The response was laconic and somewhat bewildered. Of course, I reminded myself, the La MaMa folks represented the epitome of experimental, weird, and *laissez-faire*. There was not a soul on the premises who would have said squat about the underwear on my head. They probably didn't even notice.

In my mind I began a swift mental inventory of all the places I had been, of all the smiles, the bemused faces, the joyful grins, the parting of the throngs ushering me to the head of the line. I imagined how I must have looked cycling along grinning and waving, a toddler on my back, hair streaming behind me in two wild pony tails that emerged from a pair of training pants with rosebuds on them.

There was no explaining to anyone, no erasing, no going back to regain my dignity. It was official. I was Panty-head Mama. The most striking part of the whole thing is that people seemed to love me. For the entire time I had worn underwear on my head, I had felt like a woman blessed with joy and serenity. I felt un-judged by the world, yet connected and as if all my life was seamlessly sewn together with the indestructible thread of laughter.

And now I do so cherish the memory of that day: riding home, the bike moving as if friction had been eliminated, my child with me, my head brimming with ideas and words, my basket full of great food, and the world full of love. I had felt as if those people connected to me because I made them forget themselves and they felt that wonderful absurdity that lurks inside all of us, although we often fight to keep it buttoned down.

And to this day I am convinced that panties on the head of some bitter, unhappy mom would never light up the world the way I did that day. It is an idea I hold onto as I get older and see myself as not so lush, not so attractive in the eyes of the world. But what I return to is the notion that humor keeps us feeling young, vital, and juicy beyond our years. I am the first one to make fun of myself for gaffs, I still wear silly hats, put stickers on my bike as I roll through the city streets and holler raucous "hellos" to folks I encounter. I consider it a primary résumé credential that I can make any baby laugh by virtue of my willingness to play the biggest fool.

I see that I look years younger when I am laughing, and nothing can bring on a giggle like the memory of me on my bike, rosebud panties askew with my head held high waving and peddling. I was the queen of all I surveyed, and in my laughing mind, I still am. The absurd can be so very, very divine.

LUDDITE LOVE

I am the ultimate Luddite. I love everything tactile, analog, old-fashioned, old timey. I love ticking pendulum clocks, fountain pens, high rag paper, candles, and chamber music. I love to make things, do things: pottery, dinners, knit sweaters, refinish furniture. I must have a 19th century person living somewhere within me, albeit one who likes central heating, a steaming shower, and a fast car.

There was never much hope for me to make an easy transition into the digital age. I had been an executive who was old enough to have a secretary who typed or word-processed everything I wrote with pen and paper. Who needed to learn to use a computer? I loved books, and my anti-tech rant was that I didn't want to contribute to the extinction of books by embracing newfangled electronic gadgets designed to replace libraries and words on paper. I even believed technology would be a passing obsession and I, clinging to my old ways, would seem wise for my tenacity.

Other less staunch Luddites would topple, but not me. HA! As a hedge to this fantasy, I did invest in the stock market's technological super highway, with a prescience showing I understood that the rest of the world was not like me. I also bought a computer for the house for anyone who cared to use it.

In the early 1990's, my then very young daughter wanted to help me with the damn thing, but she told me "Mama, you have bad attitude. And I am not going to help you unless you get a better grip on yourself." I wondered where she had heard those words. And so I blundered along, losing work that was eaten by the cannibalistic machine, and ever and again returning to my yellow pads and leaky pens.

When my husband's career took off, I quit my day job. He invited me to follow my dream of being a writer with one caveat: I had to learn to use the computer. He was not going to type my work. I wasn't going to inveigle my old secretary or my best friend from college or any of the other Luddite enablers who populated my last-century world.

I agreed, and threw myself at my daughter's feet. See, she comprehends my dyslexia and I can be incompetent with her. After all, I taught her to speak, walk, swim, and keep clean – she owed me. So every night, little by little, with my fierce impatience mostly in check, my girl walked me through the basics of my little, flat, blue Apple computer. She led me to the joys of email, quick edits, videophones, scanners, digital photos. And although I remain some distance from being totally competent, I do have moments when I bask in technology's glow.

She just sent me a text message this morning between her classes at Columbia and her flight to the boyfriend in San Francisco. How fast they grow up. It read, "Hey, techno wizard Mama, how's it goin'?" I started typing back letter by letter when my 17-year-old son walked in.

"Ma, what are you doing typing a letter?"

Feeling cool, I quipped, "No, I am texting."

"Not like that Ma. You have to go into the program on your phone that lets you hit a button and a choice of words comes up. Here, look, 'cause I am only going to show you once." I wanted to say, "Suppose I said that to you, you big lunk! You wouldn't be dressed right now." But I held my tongue so I could get the techno goodies.

The next time a message comes for my husband, the

self-professed geek of the family, and he pecks at the keyboard to return it, I will take the tech initiative and graciously bestow the shortcut. He is impressed whenever I figure out a new machine, reboot my computer, switch modes or… Okay, they are *all* impressed if I do any modern thing with aplomb.

And yet, it doesn't mean I don't relish an evening in candlelight and cello playing with a bottle of pre-techno wine at my feet. I am smitten with the old ways. Still, I crave the speed, connectivity and graceless efficiency of this new era. That is, until the hard drive dies or the extensive cell phone memory fails because it fell into a puddle. Then I am overjoyed with my paper phone book kept for years with pens of many colors.

Wait, I have a text coming in. It's my daughter. I can tell because I programmed my phone to play the theme from *Charlie's Angels* whenever she calls. Ahhhh, technology.

TECH TIME OUT

Is there magic afoot?   I seem to possess an unquenchable desire to understand what goes on where I cannot readily see it: in treetops, or swamps, or the well dug den under my daylilies. I am drawn to the tidy, tight little homes made by mice and birds where every stick and fluff of cotton has been meticulously chosen and placed with concentration and purpose. The well-timed return of the nesting swans in brackish waters, braving snows and floods to create homes for cygnets berates my abilities as a mother, as their steadfastness is nothing compared to my edgy ups and downs. The arrival of peepers— Chordates —whose Latin name reminds us that these tiny male amphibians sing loudly to attract mates. This is the kind of intentional activity in vernal pools, on the wing or across fields that I fret the human world is in danger of losing as we fall in thrall to technology.

The world whirls faster every year. The glut of information spewed at us through devices and media and then gobbled up by our own volition is staggering. Many of us believe that we can forestall disaster by knowing more, reading more, learning more, tuning in more frequently and falling asleep not by flickering starlight, but rather attempting to tumble into the arms of Morpheus hugged by the sickly bluish glow of electronics.

Even though hosts of stories, studies and gathered wisdom inform us, those of us who read and watch too much are aware that these habits are not healthy. It doesn't do our bodies or brains any good. And yet we persist at being plugged into technology and information at a rate as yet unseen in any generation before. It is not just the folly of the young; we all stare at screens, tweeting, texting and typing on noisy keyboards cramping our fingers and distorting our hands, while the natural world beckons and builds ceaselessly.

This is the all too ubiquitous American landscape. Small technological horizons with photographs bleeding off screens and wonders proffered by friends or colleagues to tantalize us with the life they are leading, causing us to perhaps question the mundanities of our own pedestrian existence.

But there is a glorious, free, exhilarating cure: nature, writ small or immense.

I wander out to my Hudson Valley backyard, or pull my old Raleigh three-speed over by a rock or a bench. I stop. I like to vigorously imagine that I can hear what goes on in the magical, scurrying world high up in the trees, or underground beneath layers of leaves and amid the timidly germinating bulbs. I wonder how the worms have moved through such muddy soil when it is difficult for me to pick up my feet hampered by mucky boots sinking into loamy earth. How did the pine tree dress the massive wound caused by insects? A decade ago the infestation seemed pernicious and at soil level. However, today the burl scar is high up poking at heaven's roof, bulging on the trunk of the still strong tree.

I imagine the dedicated toil of the gray mouse as she carried cotton wool up the rough wood pole and into the abandoned birdhouse. How many uncomplaining trips does it take to make a snug home? Is there singing in there after the moon dims and the coyotes cavort and chant? Yes, I am a fan of Beatrix Potter, but my magical kingdom is not a place where animals sport frocks, aprons, suspenders or tight blue waistcoats. No, for me the wild world of nature is constantly working and evolving often out of sight of humans, which is why it requires ardent imagination.

I believe this imagination needs to be cultivated in everyone. It requires only a watchful eye, a keen ear, a taste for scenery, and a belief in spirit. We need to attempt to feel the wind ruffling the feathers of the red-tailed hawk as he launches from a cliff soaring into the turbulent sky and regards the white caps on the widest expanse of the Hudson River. Does he, like me, calculate if he can make it to the next tiny island? I, in my kayak – he, on the wing. Are the nesting barn swallows put off by the curious kitten who waits at the base of their nest? If so, then their dangerous play taunting him disabuses me of that notion. A duo of fledglings swoops down, skimming the top of his furry head. He swivels left to right and topples to the ground. Would I be crazy to imagine hearing their adolescent giggles or their triumphant chatter as their mother calls them home at dusk? Do they recount this story in the comfort of the nest box, or like wild teenage boys do they clam up about their day's adventure when mom appears?

In my semi-sleep world I marvel at the singing of the foxes and wonder if a congress is held to determine what key, where the song will go and how it will end? I am beguiled by the vulpine Philip Glasslike compositions as they float past my ears on moonlit summer nights. Detached from my tether of electronics I float, beating back modern apathy as I sit in evenings on the porch, or in my hammock, or in a sturdy wooden chair carted high to a hilltop. It is as if the infinite variety of sounds is a tonic to a modern world-weary woman.

We are equally soothed by the bouquet of aromas emanating from our natural world. I gobble up the distinct smell of winter on the back of the tabby cat's fur. It is a Proustian link to my young son's buzz cut redolent with the same frosty smell. I am sure it cannot be copied. In spring the cats stop to smell tiny grape hyacinths that have been moved into the lawn by stealth underground gardeners, and they nuzzle first daffodils or sleep in lavender beds. Cats crush and aggressively snuggle the wild catnip even before it reaches an inch in height. Yet it returns and spreads and entices them into new corners of the adjacent forest because they reseed it. I am sure the wild creatures are equally drawn to aroma, otherwise why do they chose the lilies and narcissi for burrows even though the wild open fields abound? Unlike us, the wild things do not need to be persuaded to head out and bend to sniff and carefully choose bundles to put on nightstands to guard against nightmares. The enchantments of olfaction are legendary. I employ them to calm and seduce me away from the flickering screens and into the edge of wildness clinging to my technology-infected world.

In order for us to dive deeply into numinous nature we must sally forth into opulent wildness. It is joyfully present all around us. We must push back from the timely real terrors that encroach and ask us to be numb, and rather push into lofty and lavish nature.

When my children were small I entreated them to have a firmly crafted vision at the ready for the moments when they were stalked by night terrors or waking fear. I said they were to imagine a small video to play internally in order to transform a scary narrative into a calm one. Adults call for nothing less. My vision to quell and banish modern morbidity is a moment in nature. I am seated on the double bench in our property called the "way back." I am calmly attempting a meditation in late fall. The rustle and hum of birds and animals as they head home provide a susurrus to soothe me. I hear a snapping of twigs and I turn, thinking it is the cat once again attempting to surprise me. He seems to love it when I jump and shriek. Instead I am eye to eye with a big antlered buck. We both exhale and he leaps right over me. I am stock still as I see the underside of his belly, a marvel, and the bleached white tail, thicker that I thought, and his folded legs and his hooves, black patent leather shiny as if he were a

Christmas reindeer in flight. He lands. I breathe. He is gone. I am alone. We are both safe and the murmur of dusk continues.

This vision held firmly can bring me calm like no modern medication or YouTube video. I create my own halcyon world. We all can.

AN AFFAIR WITH GLOBAL WARMING

I am sitting on a bench in the back of my five acres in the Hudson Valley. I am sun and work warm from time spent traipsing across the property with a recently torn meniscus. It is happily the first day in weeks I can get out and garden.

I am trimming lavender bushes and my hands are redolent with the oily aroma. I finish and head to sit on a rough wood bench to rest my knee, which is beginning to throb. I am wearing a long-sleeved French sailor shirt; I had to push the sleeves up, because I was so warm. I sit and turn directly into the radiance and think how lovely this is, how lucky I am.

And then it hits me. It is the end of the first week of December in the Hudson Valley over a hundred miles north of New York City. There is something terribly wrong. I had been pulling out weeds easily, as there has been no killing frost, the trees are confused and start to push out buds, the onion grass is an inch high, a site normally relished in early spring. We just finished a Thanksgiving so warm that cooking for thirty was a chore, not due to the scope of guests, but because with the oven on and burners blasting for over half a day, it reduced our open plan loft to hellish hot. It was over 60 all day.

And still I leaned back to close my eyes and I breathed in the warm air and let the sun soak into my face. It felt so amazing. And I thought, what else has felt like this, so wrong, so exhilarating, and it crashed in on me: an affair. I was having an affair with Global Warming. In fact, many of us are.

I hadn't had an affair since before I was married. When I did, I was old enough to know better, in my mid 40's and so starved for affection from my babies' father that I set off to the South of France with his brother. Yes, not proud, not right, but boy was it exciting. At every turn, I pushed the wrong into a corner and embraced the race of my heart, the clench of my loins and the full throttle knowledge that this would not last, and I did nothing to stop it.

I moved on. He moved on. But I can still conjure the heat we generated. It is the same full-body frissons I felt today soaking in the sun, into much older bones and perhaps a wiser spirit. I know I have to take responsibility for my personal morality and etiquette, but what about the rest of the world?

I have ridden a bike as my main means of transportation for over 40 years. I rode home from work in labor, twice. I ride just like the postman: in rain, snow, sleet, and dark of night. We recycle. We have a wood stove with a catalytic converter that burns the smoky emissions. But we do drive a car upstate. I travel often to foreign lands. I sometimes toss catalogs in the trash in the lobby rather than hauling them upstairs to recycle. I eat meat. I love the feeling of sun on my skin. I am no eco-saint.

I don't know what else to do to combat climate change other than donate to good causes, continue on a positive path and call out climate deniers. I am not causing the sun to feel warm in December and the sky to be a scrubbed blue, which fuels my lust to remain outside longer and longer.

I hear folks everywhere exclaiming how utterly delicious the weather is. So far this is a snowless, frost-free, mild start to winter. And each one of us quickly says "great weather, but weird. It makes me uneasy." Now think, you are having an affair with Global Warming. It shatters your calm resolve when you realize that you can't sustain this level of wonder and joy. None of us can.

I want to get down to business and flirt with winter. I want to embrace the slippery sidewalks, and make hot toddies, and pile on wooly sweaters and thick mittens. I want a snow angel to follow me home to where I am enchanted by the idea of heat in my sweet abode. I want to recognize that there is no place like home, even when it is freezing and winter has stayed wrapped around me for months threatening never to leave.

A HUMAN PACKAGE, HANDLE WITH CARE

Turkish is not a language that trips off my tongue. I am fairly adroit with the Romance languages, but Turkish is touted as an impenetrable language for non-natives. However, I attempt to *say* "thank you, I appreciate you," or "please" in any country I visit. I feel it indicates respect, and although I may be clumsy, I try.

"Thanks" in Turkish is *teşekkür*. The lovely Turks say it is easy to remember – just think: tea and sugar. I kept thinking it and losing it and even wrote it on a slip of paper secreted in my pocket.

I landed in Istanbul and spent three enchanted days lost in maze-like markets, eating warm seed-covered simit bread from carts, marveling at the sunken cistern and the inverted statues, visiting the Blue Mosque, Hagia Sophia and filling my head with the *Muezzin's Ezan*, the call to prayer, echoing from every mosque's minaret, five times a day. Everyone was generous and open-hearted, helping me to boats that floated up and down the Bosporus, or to bridges traversing Asia and Europe, advising me on the most delicious food redolent of unidentifiable spices. And the meals ended with Turkish delight. I would need to say thanks, often.

I was in Turkey to write a story about the whirling dervishes, so after three days I took a puddle jumper to the interior city of Konya, the epicenter of whirling dervishes. Konya is the home of the 13th century Sufi poet Rumi, the founder of the Mevlevi sect. Rumi was also an Islamic scholar whose wisdom is beloved worldwide and he believed much of his inspiration emanated from his moving meditation practice called *Sama*. This meditation is still practiced by the Semezens or the Dervishes. It involves a solemn whirling while wearing tall felt hats and wide sun bleached white-skirted uniforms. One hand is lifted to the heavens, taking from God, and the other points down giving life to the earth. The ritual chronicles the spiritual path humanity must take to enlightenment and can involve up to 2000 continual whirls, all executed to the mesmerizing traditional music of reed flutes and drums. The importance of the Whirling Dervishes can be attested to by the fact that UNESCO has declared them international treasures as they are "Masterpieces of the Oral and Intangible Heritage of Humanity."

I had been granted not only interviews with the head of the Konya Dervishes, but also a chance to participate in dance classes being co-taught with an American modern company called Battery Dance. This was part of a U.S. State Department cultural exchange program. I felt incredibly lucky.

I settled into the Hotel Rumi (where else would one choose to stay?) and ventured across the street to Rumi's tomb -- now the Mevlana museum and cultural nexus. The tombs of Rumi and his followers were all capped with huge turbans and many worshipers were lost to prayer at this holy site. I began to think about what other wonders are hidden in and around Konya. After all, one cannot whirl for a week. And so I began to ask.

I was informed that there was an ancient church built in 500 AD, dedicated to Emperor Constantine's mother, Helena. I would have to take a few buses and hike a bit, but it would be worth it. Since I seemed miserable at whirling -- I constantly tumbled to the ground -- I decided I would have an adventure.

And here I become an unreliable narrator because try as I might to find the exact village and location of my hygira, I can't. And so it becomes ever more remarkable that I set forth and returned enlightened and unscathed.

The next morning after my thick yogurt and caramelized cherries, I pinned a note to my jacket with all the instructions, written in Turkish, about my destination. I had asked the concierge at the hotel to write down where I was going and then the reverse instructions for my trip home. This was happily before GPS and cell phones were ubiquitous. I would be a package, at the mercy of bus drivers and strangers.

I walked up to folks and showed them my note. One by one, I was escorted to the appropriate bus. I waited, and kept showing my note until the correct conveyance arrived. It never occurred to me that I could have been sent on a wild, dangerous goose chase instead of to St. Helena's church. I finally arrived after about an hour and began to trudge up a huge hill to the proffered site. A car stopped jammed full of people and offered me a ride. I showed my note, everyone nodded, and minutes later I was at a pile of rubble.

I scampered over rocks and debris and into the church; it was small, square and ancient. I sat on a rock and pondered the strange turn of events that led me to sit here in the cool quiet. I was chasing an alternative meditation since the whirling one had eluded me. There is a true sense of awe that pours over me when, in rare moments, I find myself alone in places of wonder. Here on the edges of the Silk Road, a great Emperor had built a monument to his mother, Helena. And now I sat here having arrived as a package.

I started back down the hill and encountered a young woman with a donkey fully laden with stones. I showed her my note, and as she came closer she became noticeably excited. This young stranger kept pointing to my blue eyes as she grabbed my arm and tugged me toward a small café. When the older proprietor came out, this woman also had blue eyes. I surmised it was my escort's mother. But I will never know. By then I was hungry, so when they led me to a table, I was ready to tuck in. They brought out soup and bread and a salad of unidentifiable grains. The younger woman wanted our picture. Blue eyes together, we both smiled, and I held out my money to pay for lunch. They shook their heads, but I persisted and then asked, via my note, to be returned to the bus stop for my sojourn home.

The bus arrived at my starting point and dusk fell. I arrived at the theater in time for the evening's performance of Battery Dance and the Dervishes. I retrieved my ticket from the box office and washed my face in the loo before sitting in my plush seat. During the entire day, I had done nothing but show my notes and I had been whisked from one adventure to another.

In the Sufi sect, they employ spinning to endeavor to reach a level of perfection that includes the abandonment one's *nafs* or ego. I had subordinated my ego's need to control and suggest, and my desire to talk about everything and parse the yin and yang of daily life. I had uttered only *teşekkür* all day, and that had been more than enough.

THE KINDNESS OF STRANGERS

I am rarely sick. I've always considered myself a stalwart, thickish farm girl who loves to eat and hence is inoculated by nutrition. And yet when I tumble I seem to crash deeply.

This happened to me on a trip to Norway a few years ago. I was there to write about fish. Yup, fish. Fishy culinary trends, how it is farmed, lots of fascinating things to see and munch, but then I was laid low by the most terrible, yet simple thing: a head cold.

I was little-kid sick with terrible fluids flowing from my orbitals' orifices. I recall my mother's template for ascertaining if children should stay home from school with colds. You had to say sponge. If it came out, "spudge" and your breathing labored just eking out this word, you were banished to bed. During the day and night, you were trundled out for steaming over a pot of herbs with a long fairy tale intoning in the background.

I longed for that. I couldn't breathe; I was weeping and plowing through boxes of tissues. My nose was red, my eyes were pink and the thought of boarding a plane for a quick hop from Oslo to Stavanger made my head hurt so much that I pressed my temples surreptitiously against the stonewall in the park where we were ogling the beautiful sculptures by Gustav Vigeland.

Our group was scheduled to fly the next morning, a quick 284 miles, yet I was terrified. I sensed the havoc a rapid ascent and descent would do to my already painfully blocked head. I couldn't see any way out. I hate being difficult; I am someone who might do myself harm in order not to wheedle for special treatment. And I couldn't even envision a request. "Just leave me. I'll take up residence in Oslo and work for the Nobel committee."

Or perhaps I could model for the new version of Edvard Munch's "The Scream." I wanted to lie down and get better.

I escaped to a café with a colleague to get some tea. I could breathe the fumes and sip the sweet liquid and heal for a moment. This was a young colleague, but we had bonded. She was willowy and blond and not as razor sharp as I was, or thought I was, but she was generous and lovely. After we sat down, a handsome young man came up behind her and tapped her shoulder. She swiveled and saw it was someone she knew from another time. He obviously had been a tad smitten, as his face lit up when she turned.

They chatted a bit and then he politely turned to me to inquire how I was enjoying his fine country. Of course, I just blurted out everything. I was sick, we had to fly tomorrow, and I was terrified my head was going to explode. Honestly, I think I was crazy.

He was calm, blond and chiseled and without a moment's notice he said, "I have a car, let me drive you both to Stavanger. I can show you the fjords, the magical forests and perhaps we can even see some trolls. I can share Norwegian magic with you."

"Oh no." I demurred, aching to say, "Yes, yes, yes, please." But he insisted and my young beauty accepted on our behalf.

"What just happened?" I asked when he left.

"Well, it looks as if we will be traveling overland

tomorrow. Relax, it will be fun."

Jan showed up *au point* at 8 am in a gleaming, forest green BMW. The perfect car to secret us into the deep forests, past the trolls and on to the port city of Stavanger. I stepped into the back seat with the pillow purloined from the hotel and extra socks on my freezing hands. The leather seats took me in. I rolled to my side, clutching my tissue box and was asleep before we zoomed past the Nobel Peace Center. I felt safe.

I awoke to the sound of Jan holding forth about the fjords. I sat up and it was gob-smacking. There were shear cliffs chopping into dark gray water, fir trees peppered hillsides that were draped in scree. Jan explained that the depth of the water below equals the height of the fjord above. As far down, as up. I loved that; geographic equality.

As we drove along Jan told us about the trolls inhabiting the woods. These are not the evil creatures featured in fairy tales, but rather wise protectors of the forest. There is a type of troll called *Huldrefolk*, known for being handsome and blond and yet they have long tails. Often these trolls disguise their tails in carefully tailored trousers or long dresses. I had the sense that many people believed in trolls and I could see why. These forests were so glistening and lush that they must be magically tended. I miraculously began to sense their piney aroma wafting into my clogged nasal passages. Could that be?

We continued along the coast stopping to see the sweet, wooden house where Jan had grown up. We zigged and zagged and finally pulled into a big parking lot with a tiny shack. Yikes, was he now going to sell us? Was my calm and belief in the kindness of strangers about to be shattered? No. This was a favorite of forest hikers. A shack selling sausages, hot dogs, fritters, and what can only be extolled as perhaps troll elixir because they were so delicious. Spicy and crispy, served on rolls just snatched from the oven with a yeasty tang and all dripping with strong, grainy mustard. I didn't know I needed this, but it was perfect. And it wasn't fish, which was all we had eaten for the preceding week. I attempted to grab the tab, but gallant Jan said it was his pleasure to pay and to be able to show us the real Norway. This was not malarkey or a way to get the better of someone; it was so genuine, I felt as if I had fallen into a wonderful fairytale portal. And I didn't want the spell to end.

Here I was healing in the back of a car, or feeling stronger seated on a wooden bench munching magical snacks, or craning my much less foggy head to see if perhaps that might have been a troll behind an ancient fir tree, or wait – maybe he's there by that pile of stones shining in the distance. Everything took on sheen and glint. The air seemed thinner and yet more redolent of every glorious forest aroma one could conjure. I was obviously delirious or how else to describe my joy, my clarity and my sense of health rushing back like the strong currents below us.

We pulled up to the hotel in Stavanger just as the rest of the group arrived looking bedraggled and frantic from a bad flight and a long delay. Jan waved my colleague and me off, even when we asked him to join us in the rathskeller for drinks. He was heading to visit a cousin in town. We exchanged contact information, and like the magical wizard I came to know, he vanished into the misty evening.

That night we dined, yes on fish, at the Norwegian Petroleum Museum. A wonderful eatery perched atop an oil derrick in the North Sea. The sea chopped and splashed at long legs sticking out of the modern structure and I felt better than I had in quite a while. I wondered if, in fact, Jan had been a troll. After all, we never saw Jan without his well-made trousers. We never swam or took a sauna, so perhaps he is one of the *Huldrefolk* and he was summoned to bestow his kindness on a very sick stranger.

VIRGIN THESPIAN

By the time I was 59 I had produced a multitude of theatrical events: New Year's Eve in Central Park replete with fireworks, productions on the Lincoln Center Plaza, over 60 shows a year for a decade at NYC's downtown experimental hub, La MaMa, Bicentennials in New York and L.A., as well as an opera entitled *Calling,* based on the book I wrote about my experience of 9/11. Some were glorious, some ho-hum and some soporific.

Yet, in all this time, I had never been in a play. I had never been an actor. Truth be told, often producers talk trash about actors. They need motivation, they desire an impetus, they are fragile, they need tea or Irish whiskey backstage, some moan and gnash their teeth. Others do warm-ups, which make you believe that death is just around the corner and you hope the show will go on. Others are inspired, exquisite and transform themselves into beings who carry you across space and time making you wish the curtain would never fall. I didn't understand the impetus to act – my life seemed too full of pretend and wheedling and cajoling already. I didn't want to add acting to my repertory.

So when an email wafted over my transom with the message, "Looking for non-actors" to take part in a play presented by a well-known Swiss company under the aegis of Performing Space 122, a respected downtown venue, I thought, "should I audition?" Why did I think that? Well, my 60th birthday was fast approaching and I love a challenge. One of my favorite gifts to myself is to do something I have never done. A new place, a new experience, lights me up. So I rode my bike all the way to Fifth Avenue and 82nd Street to the Goethe-Institut and I had my first audition.

I found out there was no script. It was an immersive production. Luckily, I knew what that was. Heck, La MaMa had been a pioneer in that type of work. In immersive, the lines between the audience and the production are blurred until often, one merges with the other. When I was Executive Director at La MaMa in the '80s we presented a version of three Greek plays directed by the wildly talented Andrei Serban with music by Liz Swados. The audience was swirled into the hubbub as *The Trojan Women* were enslaved and tortured. The play was lit only by torches, and the chanting in ancient Greek was mesmerizing and to some, terrifying. We received a letter from a woman who swore that she was driven crazy by the experience. I surmised she had her own transportation well before the show, but I wrote her a lovely letter. Before I buckled down to write her, I asked the Managing Director if he would authorize an expense so I could send a hive of live bees to this terrified curmudgeon. I was kidding; he turned down my request. Ahhh, checks and balances.

I liked the director, Dominic Huber. He carefully explained his concepts about the work called *Hotel Savoy*. It was based on a 1924 novel by the Austrian Joseph Roth and would involve a series of installations where the audience would move from one spooky environment to the next. The audience was ushered in, one-by-one, every 6 minutes, as to be separated from companions and familiar faces. An empty hotel provided the backdrop for this scary habitat. The space was glorious. An old mansion with a winding staircase, a rickety elevator, high ceilings, rubbed wood paneling and a *soupçon* of spooky neglect.

I sort of understood the gist of the work. I wasn't auditioning for any particular role. I think Huber wanted to see what characters might fit best with the people who showed up, hoping we could speak extemporaneously, in a fluid enough way to carry off improvised conversation, six minutes at a time, for two one-hour long shows each night. I didn't care if I got this gig or not. Thus armed with indifference, I was awarded a role. I was to be the bartender.

They wanted me to mime serving drinks and I put my foot down. I was no method actor. I would cut lemons and pour vodka over ice and ply my customers with a proper drink for our six-minute interlude. At that point, a secret buzzer would sound and I had a breezy minute to get the customer to the next location. Swiss watch precision. My task was to send my audience member on to the chatty barber, my new best friend. In would waltz my next victim.

I encountered R, hairdresser to the stars, inventor of the shag haircut and proprietor at Fleuremedy, on the first day of rehearsal. We couldn't miss each other. We were the only grownups in the room. R is all swagger and artifice, but so loving with his posh British "Daaaahlings," interspersed with his original cockney twang that poked out every so often. I immediately loved him. At our first break he took me onto the balcony where he insisted we smoke a little pot. Honey, this was horse tranquilizer strong. Time stood still and the environment, which had been a tad weird, took on the demeanor of a Stephen King novel, and I embraced it. After that moment R regaled me with tales of the women and men in his life. I knew inside stories about movie stars and politicians and all the folks in between. R took over cutting my hair and not for his normal $750 fee, but for lunch or whatever extra cash I had.

He led the cast through wonderful pre-show meditations and at our breaks between shows he and I would smoke another joint. I was never much of a smoker or drinker, but with R, and high above the MET museum pretending to be an actor, it all seemed so right. I would be my own diva.

The shows were exhausting. Two hours of back-to-back, non-stop improvised conversation within a framework. I had to talk about the idea of being trapped. Where did we all want to go? Did anyone really get out and on with their lives? That sort of thing for six minutes, then hit restart and do it again.

As I rode my bike home in the wonderful New York City autumn air, with big shadows and a new found slight chill, I thought "Who knew acting was so hard?" I would then laugh out loud, perhaps still under the spell of R's magic potions, and continue to peddle home. When I arrived all I wanted was silence. Don't ask about my day, about the show. Quiet, maybe TV, or a book. But, honestly I was talked out. I think my husband relished the six-week run.

On the night *The New York Times* reviewer came, everyone was nervous. When he walked into my bar, I immediately recognized his grumpy countenance and insisted he needed a drink, maybe two. We connected and in his review I was referred to as "the genial bartender." And I might add, I was the only character referred to in a positive light. Glad I fought for real vodka and lemons.[1]

When our run was over there was a momentary flurry of conversation about remounting the show in Europe, and we shared excitement based on nothing other than balderdash. I knew it wouldn't happen. I had worn the producer's hat too long to have that sort of smoke blown at me.

---

[1] Charles Isherwood. "The Porter Will Kindly Show You to Your Doom." Review of *Hotel Savoy,* by Dominic Huber. *The New York Times,* October 6, 2010.

Right after my 60th birthday, I annotated my insane list of jobs: teacher, waitress, stockbroker, writer, mother, stage manager, producer and one-time actor.

I'D EAT A TODDLER

When my daughter was only four years old she began asking pointed questions about eating animals. I had begun to postulate that she was too bright for me to raise and I constantly searched for backup. That never came in the form of her biological father, a handsome, narcissistic, undereducated, lout of a man from the North Woods. When Willi asked him how animals were killed he blithely launched into how sometimes on the farm they bashed in the heads of the larger animals. He devolved from there in gristly detail...

By the time I returned home from work (remember, he thought about work while I actually worked), my pink-cheeked cherub was a vegetarian. She had ruminated and posed an additional bonus question: "Are the animals afraid when they die? And if so do we eat the fear?" Ugh, I was in way over my head.

So I bought a book on how to cook vegetarian food for growing minds and bodies. And although I never went to the plant side, I did learn food combinations and happily embraced my mother's Italian roots, which makes vegetarian food glorious and easy. And so we moved forward, often with me cooking, serving, and cleaning up from two distinct meals.

Time moved forward. I left the lout. I married a wonderful man who not only worked, but shopped for groceries and did dishes and loved my cooking. My daughter kept growing. She had a brother now who seemed to be a devoted carnivore and so I kept cooking multiple meals.

One argument my daughter and I had when she was an early teen centered on why it was wrong to eat meat. She posited that pigs were as smart as three-year-olds. Undaunted, I snapped back, "I'd eat a toddler." It was just a way to end the conversation and channel an original Irish, smart-ass Jonathan Swift who in 1729 wrote "A Modest Proposal For Preventing the Children of Poor People From Being a Burden to Their Parents or Country, and For making them Beneficial to the Publick" (sic). His idea was to utilize satire to highlight the heartless British attitude toward the Irish. My motives were less deep. I just wanted her to stop yammering at me.

Later as she navigated her way to a PhD in Sociology she told me that the "I'd Eat A Toddler" moment, as she called it, was when she knew that I was funny and perhaps a little ruthless. She is correct on both counts. When I get a head of steam up, what my father called "getting my Irish on," I imagine that I can and will do anything, and I have been known to blurt. But, while I have been very hungry, very angry, and wildly disappointed, I have never wanted to eat a sweet-faced toddler. Don't tell her 'cause it sure did shut her up.

HEIR A PARENT

"Making the decision to have a child -- it is momentous. It is to decide forever to have your heart go walking around outside your body. "

Elizabeth Stone

TO HAVE OR TO HAVE NOT

I sat on a blanket in Riverside Park with a woman friend who was hysterical over her twenty-something son's first shrink visit. The kid had not left the apartment for six months and yet kept his job as a coder, and she was at her wit's end.

I inquired, "if you had it to do over, would you have kids?"

Her answer was quick and clean.

"No,

I never wanted them.

My husband talked me into it and then he died."

I have no excuse. I sought them out. No one talked me into it. I wanted kids since I was 15. I was the neighborhood champion babysitter, at fifty cents an hour, often pretending they were my own sweet playthings.

I was so desirous of my own babies that when at 34 I found myself pregnant again, for the fourth time, after assiduously employing birth control, I decided to have this baby. The man I was with, and had been with for eight years, was a handsome asshole. No job, no desire for a career, just wanted to bed women and get trinkets for it. Yes, perfect father material.

And so I had my daughter, then my son, then left the wretched man. Then married the love of my life. And weathered the bumps, tears, clawing sadness and finally adult children who just seem to pretty much resent me.

I know I am not a middle-of-the-road choice. I was and still am an unusual person. My son reminded me this past weekend that I never used seat belts in the back seat when they were little. I know there is a scrolling list of all my parental misdemeanors. He also told me as I was fixing him breakfast – he was visiting the country house – that I needed to "stop talking." This was reminiscent of my father's admonishment to me that my only problem was that I thought too much, and compounded it by talking about it.

My kids, on occasion, impose a moratorium on talking to me, or seeing me. If I ask why or inquire how I could be a better parent at this point in their lives, they are mostly mute and mumble something about space or that I am too fast, too bouncy.

I adored having baby children, toddlers and petulant teens. I am an expert at non-verbal communication and impromptu games, baking, bed jumping, ice cream for dinner or roast chickens and mashed potatoes. I can read stories 'til the cows come home, I will unabashedly answer any questions about sex or boys or girls or finance and rarely lose my patience in those arenas. Yes, I admit I can be frustrating with my inabilities at the modern tech world, or my easy-to-ignite temper, but I see myself as generous, loyal and unflaggingly willing to help my kids and nearly anyone in their circle. And yet I still see myself reflected by them as wildly annoying. I don't want that vision of myself.

I see other parents who were unrepentant drunks all through careening childhoods and yet, their kids embrace them as wonders of the world, as they are now sober. I marvel at the kindness and closeness of those parents and their children and I yearn for that forgiveness.

Let's be honest, other than stealing the stuff, the scandal, giving them a terrible birth father, I really did work, and I tried so hard. Trips, camp, lessons, tutors, birthday parties and prom-dresses, suits and bikes. Teaching them to ski, skate, ride horses, drive stick shift, change a tire, mend a broken heart, edit papers, write poetry, make pasta sauce, roast chickens, turn simple things into beautiful things and open your heart, your wallet and your doors wider and wider. But it is seemingly not enough and in the end it breaks my heart, and so I wonder.

Would I have been better off, safer, saner, kinder, happier, if I had not had children? Would I have missed the times when I dipped my feet and hands daily into childhood magic? My aching heart says, "yes," I would have. But to inch into old age questioning what a poor job I did at mothering, and to see the results flung at me in every all-too-frequent fight, makes me want to hide or stop trying.

I can't. I can't stop trying to help with funds, or fun, or an ear, or a suggestion. Are there meetings called "Mothers Anonymous"? My life has become *unmanageable* because of the guilt I feel at not providing my two babies with a calmer, more secure, less experimental childhood. I wish there were. I can't go back and unbirth the really beautiful, smart, anxiety-filled children I have. I do question, if knowing what I know now, would I do it again?

My very selfish answer is: Yes!

Yes, because having children is an emotional, in-the-moment decision. We then spend a lifetime attempting to justify, rectify and assuage all the mistakes we made when, so full of hope, we jumped into that alluring pool of magic.

WANTED AT ANY AGE

My son Henry, a mere two weeks into his sixteenth year, decided that he does want to have kids after all. He believes kids make you less lonely. But he doesn't desire a baby – he'd like to adopt a 15-year-old. "You know mom, a kid who is at that difficult stage, not some mushy baby."

I wondered if he had chosen the age from which he had just emerged because he unconsciously acknowledges that he was in a tough phase. Is this his way of saying to me, and perhaps to himself, that he has rounded the corner at 16 and feels as if he cleared a hurdle? That 15 was a difficult age, but now he is on a more mature path?

Did he say it to make me realize he understands, in even a small way, how almost impossible it is to offer love to someone who is pushing you away? There is not a windfall of outright appreciation and love from teenagers to parents and vice versa. In fact, there is such a dearth of recognition that even my fantasies have reconfigured. Daydreaming no longer involves romance, being whisked away or lavished. Now my big fantasy involves gratitude.

In these imagined moments, my family realizes what I have done for them. They don't necessarily tell me I am wonderful. It's more a simple "Wow, you gave me a lot of attention, time, love, confidence." Some sort of reflective statement that lets me know it was all worthwhile.

I also fantasize that my brother will stop berating me for how I care for our father, and instead thank me. My ex would say, "Hey, these kids are great. You did that with no help from me. I'm sorry I couldn't be there for you, but I am an emotional cripple and chronically unemployed and this is my only lucid moment in three decades, and I want to thank you."

So when Henry said he wanted to adopt a difficult 15-year-old, I saw a spark of gratitude in him. Because after all, by staying with our kids when they are smelly or diffident, confused or rageful, aren't we recommitting ourselves to their cause? Don't we say to them, when we make endless conversation that elicits one-word responses, "we are still in here pitching"? I believe we do. Yet there were moments when I thought, "why didn't I throw him out when I could still lift him?" Now it would be at least a solid year of weight lifting before I could heave Henry out a window. But by that time, I wouldn't be angry anymore and what would I do with all those muscles? Become a bar bouncer? I can see it now, a headline reading, "Menopausal Mom Muscles Men for Money."

I also see so much of my own middle age neediness in Henry's desire to adopt another human in their difficult, unappealing time. Henry's subcutaneous wish to be loved in cranky times is so poignant to me, because in my menopausal moments, my hormonal storms, I, too, feel as if no one would want to adopt me, fall in love with me, or have an affair with me. And isn't that what we all crave? We all want to be desired in our worst moments, not just our shining bursts. We want someone to say "I would marry you again—bald, chubbier, with more money, but less energy."

So in order to proffer commitment to my kids during the rocky times, I prefer to keep the conversational ball rolling and attempt to ignore the curt answers and pretend that my one-sided jabber is actual talk. And I am astonished when at times the words begin to flow as Henry talks about books he is reading, or a teacher who is enlightened or heinous. He jokes now about the muscles he is building from all his tennis workouts. He tells me in a sidewinder way about some girl he likes, how weird he finds it when they apply masks of make-up or obsess about being skinny. He talks to me about the lost ban on assault weapons, political agendas, and hip-hop. I feel anointed by his attention.

I am beginning to see who he may become as a man and it heartens me. And although at 14 and 15 he talked about how much he hated kids, how stupid it was to have them, and how annoying they were, he now makes a grand pronouncement that he could see adopting a difficult teen.

If I knew I would get my Henry at 16, so open-hearted, funny, intense and sarcastic, I suppose I would have adopted him at 15. But instead, I got him as a mushy, giggly baby and so, by the time he hit difficult, it was too late for me to toss him out. I was sunk in love with him and all he is. I think my ability to love him makes me believe that I too, in my not as cute, not as speedy, sometimes morose and nervous middle age, am still deserving of love. We all want to be adopted over and over again.

PARENT TO THE PARENT

My father is hugging ninety and has always been what is charitably referred to as "a character." He has watery blue eyes, a shock of snow-white hair and the body of an old Irish boxer. In fact, although his work was being a journalist, he boxed, wrestled, and tussled with demons both endowed and augmented by his alcoholism.

He was a high school dropout, too smart and mouthy (an Irish curse), for early twentieth century education. He struck out on his own to be a copy boy and rose to be an on-air reporter for NBC News. He was a writer, editor and a well-known tyrant around the newsroom at 30 Rock. He dismissed all of the upper echelon brass at the network as rabbits who needed to hustle back into their hutches and "get the fuck off his news floor" – and they did. He never suffered fools lightly.

As a father, he was tough. He called my younger, gay brother "Lucy" during much of our childhood. He called me, his never slim daughter, "the southbound end of a northbound bus." He used to ask me if he could borrow my face, "I want to fight a bulldog." He thought all of this was funny and perhaps character-building. It did sadly teach me to search out men as partners who would further belittle me and call it love.

It was bittersweet after my mother passed and it became evident that I had to step up and be the support person in his life. I attempted to get him to move back north, found an apartment and was all set to relocate him. When I arrived in Durham for the move he sat me down and said, "Ducks, I know you mean well, but hell, I hate people and I don't want to move near them. I want to stay here. And besides, your mother lives in the teacups and when I can't find things I yell at her." I understood. Even in my mid-fifties I couldn't imagine relearning where everything goes and I actually craving contact with people. He had no incentive to move.

We talked and I reminded him that we wouldn't be able to get down for every holiday. He looked at me horror-stricken. "Did you think I would want that?" No, I didn't. It is what I would want and hope for from my kids, but I knew him, he wanted the couch, some food and the news. He made me promise I would fight to let him finish his life in his own house. He told me it might take a while because, "God is a woman and she is mad at me. She took your mother but left me here."

I demurred and then in a new-agey fashion retorted, "Well, *She* has lots of reason to be mad at you. You were one difficult man. What about amends?" He rolled his icy eyes and shoved a meaty paw through his thatch of white hair and barked, "That's a crock of horseshit!"

We went on like this for nearly four years. I visited or the whole family did. I cooked and he napped or watched the news. The kids would ask, "Does Grandpa really want us here?" "This is just his way," I would answer, always feeling I needed another dose of therapy. After my mother passed, he never sent a birthday or holiday card and never called. If I phoned, he was happy to chat for under five minutes. He always ended saying he sent his fondest love to Zach, my husband, and the kids, but he didn't want to talk to them. He wanted to be left alone.

His regular contact was with Rose, the housekeeper, who came, seemed to hit the restore button and leave massive amounts of food and get out of Dodge. Rose lovingly named my father "Butthead" and to anyone who had met him, it seemed like the best moniker. He is the most stubborn, hardheaded man I have ever met. He hollers, "Rose, is that you? When are you leaving?"

She yells back, "Hey Butthead, I left eggs and biscuits on the table and am taking the trash." Lately, she says he adds, "I love you, Rose, now shut the door." This is a major emotional leap for him.

This past November, on a Saturday before Thanksgiving, he fell and didn't have the strength to get up. I happened to be down in Durham visiting him. He scrambled around, knocked over some furniture and then hollered for me. I came into his room and he looked for all the world like a beached whale unable to get where he desired – he was stuck on the carpet and I was unable to get his large, slippery mammal self off the beach and back into the water, his bed.

So we sat on the floor for a long while. He composed himself and we both caught our breath. We talked about options as the wind whipped around the house. I blurted out, asking if he was ready to die, and he replied with characteristic sharp snap,

"I feel as if I am a long way from dying."

"Okay, then we need to get you some help."

"No help, no hospital."

"Well then, our only other choice is to sit here and that won't be pretty."

"Okay, call the ambulance."

We had reached a place of honesty. "No bullshit, Ducks, no bullshit. Just the facts."

It was reminiscent of the interactions I had with my kids when they were little. They would protest that they didn't want to wear coats. Instead of wheedling, I would acquiesce. "Okay, no coats." I'd carry the coat downstairs and lo and behold, once we hit the frigid street they'd shiver and cry, "Oh, Mama, so cold. Coat, please."

I believe stubbornness is a dominant familial gene: my father was ready for his coat. I called the medics. When they were about to wheel my dad out he asked for his big bag of black jellybeans and licorice sticks, his "medicine" as he called it. He also asked for a stack of magazines, *The Economist* and *Newsweek* – basic necessities. I followed behind the ambulance to the ER and we began a new journey where I was the mother to my father.

After a long Saturday night and three obligatory days of hospital stay, Medicare kicked in and my father was eligible for a rehabilitation facility. The doctors were skeptical because my dad was so debilitated from sitting around eating jelly beans and egg sandwiches, but I gave my dad a pep talk and informed him that if he worked and got his legs back, I was on board for him to go back home.

The social workers in the hospital were wizards. They found him a great sunny place on a hill across from Duke University and I was in good spirits believing perhaps he could regain the ability to walk steadily enough to motor back and forth to the bathroom and kitchen to avoid any embarrassing accidents. But when he arrived in the wheelchair van, all slumped over with his new red and black checked jacket draped over his shoulders, I felt deflated. And it only descended from there.

I had been a pretty good advocate for him. I had said with pride that he took no medicine, didn't wear glasses and lived alone since my mother died four years earlier. He was deaf and didn't want to get a hearing aid, but I am blessed with a loud clear voice and made myself heard. But his mental and physical situation had really degraded in the last month and by the time he landed in the rehab center, he just seemed hollow. He arrived with wet pants because they had left him in the van while they moved another man. The driver said he had asked to go to the bathroom but they were already in the van, so he had another accident. It is so sad, this second childhood. It is much more tragic than the first one.

All this trial and error is emboldening and joyful for a toddler, but I don't know if I have the inner reserve to actually be the parent to my own father. It is hard to change his sweat pants and see his shiny, paper thin white skin. It is sad to see him flipped and inventoried by health care workers who ask me about this scar, or this cut, bruise or mark. They are not my map. I know so little of what happened to him in his past. He isn't me, he isn't my child and so most of his life's scars were garnered without me.

Today, I stood by the side of my father's new bed in a small room high on a North Carolina hill, nine hours away by car from where my family lives and I watched him heave in and out of his bed being tended to by strangers who seemed very Southern.

In an intake interview the charge nurse held up his copy of *US News and World Report* and asked my father who was the man on the cover.

"The president'" my father tersely replied. "Do you know his name?"

"Yes BUSH, George Fuck-head Bush!"

"We don't talk like that there," the nurse snipped.

"Well, maybe you red-necks should, then he wouldn't have been re-elected, now you're stuck with him"

He gave his political jab and quickly turned away and feigned sleep leaving the nurse gasping to comprehend this man. I went out and explained to her that he was a newspaperman for forty years and a sailor before that. Thus, his behavior and speech patterns would not be reformed now with admonishments. She backed off.

When my kids were pre-teens they were gob-smacked by my father's constant swearing. My son said, "You know if Grandpa were young today he would have been a rapper, cause that's a place where swearing would be good in a job." I told my son that my first sentence was, "Where are my Goddamn lollipops?" I had learned if you wanted an emphatic reaction you needed to add invective. I was just over two years old. My father loved this; my prim mom was appalled.

But as I drove away from the nursing home I thought, "who will protect him when I am not here?

Who will take care of my family while I am here with him?

Who will do my work while I am here?"

And so I am stuck in the middle. I have bought into the belief that I can have it all. And just when I am feeling the burdens of my own age, when I am struggling to pay for college and pondering what retirement will be like for an independent worker who has no pension and slight savings, I have to contend with being the parent to my dad.

I just spoke to Rose, who drawls, "Ah, Butthead is fine. He's swearing a lot that let' me know he is him." She says I shouldn't feel as if I did anything other than right by him because he was falling and couldn't breathe so well even though he kept saying,

"I don't think I am doing poorly."

Rose would say, "You are having powerful trouble breathing, Butthead, but you don't like to listen."

"I am?" he would reply.

"Yes! You are having trouble, but you have to see it yourself." Rose is like a redneck Buddha.

I had to agree. My father – Butthead, William James Boyle, Willy-Jim, Billy Boyle of NBC News or my daddy drunk or divine – was in trouble and making bad decisions. And as much as I promised he could stay home and live out his days he was having more and more insurmountable difficulty. And so we are taking little steps toward another life for him. If he can learn to be steady on his feet and walk around the assisted living facility and make it to the john on time, then he can come home. I am praying for that to happen.

If it doesn't then I will have to negotiate another scenario.

I felt sadder and emptier leaving him to drive home than when I left my daughter, slightly miserable in her first college dorm room. She wanted to be grown and to whiz magically through college and arrive in a witch-like blink at young adulthood, but she needs to be at college to achieve that autonomy. My father needs to find his way again, learn to carry his weight in his legs and find balance or he needs to resign himself to staying in this sunny place.

As for me, this has strengthened my resolve to have a real bag of actual pills, not jellybeans that I can access with a good bottle of champagne when I choose to shuffle off. I am thinking that if I last until my father's age I still have 35 years to write, chat, weep, cook and look at cloud-swept skies and marvel at where I might transmigrate.

AMERICAN DREAM

I have a proposal. It's a simple one. But it has great potential to improve society. Let's look at some facts: A mom attempts to get child support from a deadbeat dad who evades, wheedles, and ignores her and court orders. The government wants to deport the hardworking immigrants who are actually helping the mom make it through the workweek. Who is more valuable to our country and our economy, the deadbeat dads or the hard-working immigrants?

Lately, we have seen throngs of immigrants take to the streets, parks and avenues protesting their right to remain hard-working contributors to The American Dream. We all have our own relationship with immigrants, both recent and from long ago. Unless we are a pure Native American family, we all migrated from somewhere.

We don't, however, see the non-paying deadbeat parents protest their rights, when they visit their children, attend graduations, and have holiday meals without paying child support. FYI: New York State has two separate courts, one for child support, the other for visitation, so that the parent with whom the kids live, called the "custodial parent," can't dangle visitation in an attempt to be paid the often measly sum she is owed in child support.

I am attempting to be fair calling them deadbeat parents, but I am only paying lip service because men can leave even before the kid is born. Much more often women are left to raise, care and pay for their children. And the deadbeats march to their own selfish drumbeat.

I have had a solid relationship with a woman named Aggie from the Dominican Republic. She has worked with me for 17 years, depending on the vicissitudes of finances. Meaning I have seen Aggie weekly or maybe only twice a year, but we are a cleaning, washing team. Aggie has been a remarkable, solid, calm, joyful presence in my life throughout turbulent and loving times. She stayed by my side during the heinous breakup of my relationship with the deadbeat father of my kids, and celebrated my marriage to the man who would become their "daddy" and my life's love. She loves our kids and cats and gets them all to give her *besitos* and even believes they speak *Espanish*.

Aggie is the hardest working, most scrupulous person I have ever encountered. If she says she will do something, she will. If she needs to miss work, she calls. She works long hours, takes initiative, and I offer her raises and am happy to report I found her other residents who enjoy her services. It was Aggie who asked to be paid "on the books" and to have taxes withheld. It was Aggie who attended a class to become a citizen, a word that is still difficult for her to pronounce. And in April she succeeded and was promoted to full citizen of the United States.

My deadbeat ex is, in my mother-in-law's parlance "a no-excuse white man." His lineage traces back to the Mayflower, he attended private undergraduate college and has an Ivy League MBA. He is handsome, upright and chronically unemployed. And he is, in a friend's words, "mean as cat shit." You can't invent these monikers, so it is best to attribute and marvel at the verbiage.

This man has never paid child support in a timely manner. When he first left, before we had a written agreement, he never paid, and never filled the refrigerator. His first assigned payment was $50 a week toward the support of two kids in NYC. At the time my gay, black babysitter said (and please embellish this with all the drama and sibilance you can muster), "What am I supposed to do with that? Rent a video and buy a bag of chips?"

His payments were sporadic and still made the kids travel to his hovel-like apartment where he occupied one room shared with another man and they all slept in one bed or the kids on a mattress. This blue blood scion of pilgrims still kept up the pretense that he would soon be rich and buy the kids anything they wanted. After five years, he stopped pretending to work as a real estate agent and moved back up to the Adirondack Mountains where his mother was well placed and could assist in getting him employment and an apartment with more than one room.

I joked that he was repatriated like the wolves to Yellowstone, but then wolves only kill what they really need to survive. My kids kept taking the eight-hour bus ride back and forth for holidays but he didn't pay. On occasion my husband and I bought plane tickets because it seemed so punitive to have them on a bus for such a long haul, especially for short breaks like Thanksgiving. Over time my daughter stopped going, but my son, ever the rescuer, keeps at it.

When our daughter was accepted to an Ivy League school this deadbeat first tried to talk her into attending community college and then transferring to save money. When I attempted to enforce the agreement we signed which stipulated that each party was responsible for half of all educational expenses, he went to court, armed with the expensive lawyer that I assume was paid for by his mommy. Imagine this: he won. He never has to pay anything toward his children's education because his lawyer argued and won. The winning argument centered on the agreement we signed when he left. It reads, "Each party shall be responsible for half of the children's educational expenses." His lawyer argued tuition was not an educational expense, only books are.

I had been operating in Family Court as my own lawyer, *pro se*, I couldn't justify paying a lawyer when I had to buy school clothes, books, tuition. You get the point. I appealed; I still lost. Our daughter graduated *magna cum laude*. She did not invite him to graduation; it is everyone's loss.

His mother pays for his apartment. He shows no income on the books so New York State cannot get him for child support. I have a stack of judgments attesting to his debt and New York State even attaches interest: nine percent, a whopping return on investment. But these judgments are worthless.

As a kid, I recall my father returning from some assignment overseas. He was covering a junta. I don't remember where, but he came home with a suitcase filled with cash. We were so excited. He told us it was worthless, the country had become something else and this currency was no longer, well, current. So we played Monopoly with it until one night he took all the cash and wallpapered the tiny garage bathroom with it. I have thought about doing a wall in judgments but court papers are not pretty like currency and it would be a very sad powder room.

One day Aggie and I had a discussion on immigration and she wondered why this country wouldn't want more hard-working people like her. I concurred. Later when I relayed the exchange to my daughter, a very political Columbia student, she had a brilliant, subversive idea: "How come they want to deport the people like Aggie who actually contribute to this country? Why don't they consider getting rid of all the fathers who don't pay child support and hide their income or, worse, have their mothers support them?"

Ah, there's an idea. I'd love to be on the dock

when that ship departs. The men – okay, I'd include the women, too – who don't pay child support for their offspring would be loaded on board. The ship would be packed to the gunwales with those who think the country, their ex-spouses, the world owes them a living and they have to do nothing to receive the tender glow of their children's love. I can see the boats pulling away taking this cargo of deadbeat, ne'er-do-wells into the sunset. The ship would sail to a distant shore and off-load this cargo of non-contributors while back in America, the immigrants' hardened hands curled around plows, mops, or those perched in trees, or crouched picking crops, would ascend to their rightful place in The American Dream.

TIME IS A JET PLANE

This past week my family, all four of us, worked at fever pitch on various deadlines. My daughter, visiting from college, stayed up late to finish her thesis. I was on deadline for a bundle of stories and my husband, Zachary, was in production fury. My son, Henry, was in the throes of his final high-school project, his senior presentation for physics – a conceit which postulated that this slippery science could improve his pool game.

Our house hummed. Henry and I rose at dawn, our natural bright time, while my husband and daughter slept late after having tumbled into bed as trash trucks clattered below our downtown loft. We were once again all together, and I kept breathing in the scent of our rare, sweet, four-cornered existence.

Time seems to be racing since my children morphed into at least quasi-adult beings. I wonder, does time accelerate as you age or does the advent of grown children only make it appear that way? I hope it is an illusion, like the way modern car mirrors make it seem as if every Mini-Cooper is a looming SUV.

This sped-up time is also wreaking havoc with my emotional life. Maybe interior life can only handle one speed and if we push it too fast, it buckles, causing tears and terrible waves of terror and bittersweet commotion. I have always been emotional, but this is different. This page that I'm about to flip, on which my children return to my nest only occasionally, is monumental. Not for them but for me.

On the morning of Henry's big presentation he and I were once again up in the soft gray near-light. We reviewed his notes cards, ate big bowls of berries, and he scurried to pack up his giant poster board, pasted with pictures and captions designed to provide the perfect backdrop to any presentation. He also had crammed in a miniature pool set, which mingled with crumpled papers overflowing from his backpack.

"Hey, why don't I drive you to school?" I offered. He declined. Henry's first response is usually "no," but he often reconsiders. So I wasn't surprised when ten minutes he later he asked if the offer was still good.

By then I had settled into writing and really didn't want to brave the messy bedroom and my sleeping husband to find clothes, but I thought to myself, "Okay, take the kid." We corralled my son's gear, walked to the garage, and plopped everything into the car. There he was, well over 6 feet tall, clean-shaven, neat in the way that giant hip-hop clothes can be. "Okay, Ma, let's go – you know I like to be early."

I looked at him, at us, at the poster covering the back seat, the gear, the soon-to-be detritus of high school, and I burst out miserably, "This is the last time I will ever drive you to school, with a project, this is the last time –"

"—Hey, Ma, I am not dying. You know these moments are more a parent thing than the kinda' stuff kids think about."

I knew, I know, and I hadn't planned to make this drive a monumental marker. I had made a hapless offer, and in one fell swoop, it became, oh my God, a huge moment, a milestone. We were here together, me in my mother moment and he ready to roll. Me saying, "wow, this is so fast" and Henry raucous and ready, chafing at the necessities of his final high-school task.

Back home alone I stowed the car and wandered for a moment, not wanting to dive back into work. I felt so full, crammed with vibrations of what I've missed in my life. I feel I stumbled mindlessly through too many moments, later gawking at the wonders I allowed to blow past. Today I wanted to save this nugget.

I walked across the street having decided to splurge on coffee someone else made. I pushed open the squeaky screen door of the coffee shop and the music hit me.

Bob Dylan is singing, filling me with music from when I didn't know any better. His croaky voice breaks, and I hear it loud and clear: *"Time is a jet plane, it moves too fast."* I know this song from 1975, it's "You're a Big Girl Now."

I am. I am a big girl now, and one who would really like to get off the jet and find a way to slow the roll of time barreling over me. But work, family, and life beckon so I better get back on my jet and tackle the day.

FRAGILE FABRIC

Marcel Proust wrote gloriously and penned the belief that memory lives, really vibrates, in the senses. The taste from the now iconic Madeleine cookie unlocked memories for Proust's protagonist, leaving all of us longing for crumbs of a magical confection that might do the same.

When my mother died I found no wizardry in tastes, smells, or the feel of her artifacts like jewelry or her French copper cooking pans. What I found is that my memories of her are stitched and woven into her clothes. Fabric holds the key to remembrance. For me, fabric unlocks memory from my overwrought brain and drapes me in images, tastes, smells, and entire days.

The task of excavating my mother's closets and drawers fell to me and her sixteen-year-old granddaughter – my girl, Willi. We spent hours immersed in the veil of Norell perfume, digging back in time to Fracas, and Shalimar. The bottles and scents moved me, but I remained rooted in the 21st century. It was the touch of silk from Hong Kong, cashmere from France, or a quilt made from my grandfather's old dress shirts that sent frissons of memory down my arms and up my legs, landing in my center.

I had a relationship with my mother that was fraught with expectation. She expected me to be more like her and I was more like my father. I was a tomboy, a pony rider, a tussler, a girl who chopped off her long hair at camp and sent it home in a box, a young woman who wanted no part of my mother's Chanel suits or pave diamond rings. I wanted independence, education, travel and to be stronger than any boy in the class.

My mother told me I was beautiful and a wonderment, but also divulged her terror of me as I lay in her arms wailing. I was born tongue-tied and cried, starving from the minute I was wrestled out of my mother's womb until days later when my mother argued with the doctors that there was something really wrong with me, and no, I was not just a *lazy* baby!

I have been hungry ever since. Hungry for words, for tastes, for experiences, and for freedom. Perhaps when they cut my stuck tongue, my mother felt me prepare myself for this intense independence. It was difficult for me as an adolescent and as a young woman to express to my mother that I loved her because I was so busy on my own hell-bent, new found feminist track. I was vibrating in a whirligig of activity designed to prove how unlike any woman of my mother's generation I was, and how like myself I had become.

This morning I lay, half awake, in my bed piled high with crisp sheets, a patchwork quilt and a lemon-yellow mohair throw. I was insulated, in a protective cocoon, or so I thought, but memory is insidious and stealthy. In a mental flash I began tidying my daughter's room (mind you, this is only fantasy). I was folding clothes and I picked up a piece of purple I knew my daughter didn't own. I closed my eyes and looked deeper, it was a shawl made of purple fabric embroidered with gold and red that my mother had worn over her shoulders in the '50s or '60s. Where had that vision come from? Where had that swatch of fabric been stored until now when it flew out of my brain and re-knit itself to a dream that was shoved into my daughter's dresser?

I realize there is a tenuous connection at best between my memories and the fabrics they are sewn to. The texture, colors, and patterns hold intricate memory jolts.

My mother loved to sew, she adored fabric and crafted many mother-daughter outfits for us. One Easter she made aprons for a late fifties egg hunt. I use her apron now, and each time I brush by it in the kitchen drawer I am reminded of an incredible time where a woman with an Anthropology degree from Wellesley College, who had done her Honors Thesis on Peyote, reveled in a party where she and her rebellious daughter wore matching aprons. More cultural backstory is told by those aprons than reams of sociology. I wear her apron now, unironed and tied around a pair of stovepipe straight trousers and a black silk shirt as I assemble dinners for guests in my TriBeCa loft. I never thought I'd use it, but the ability to grab and wipe, to not worry about splashes and spills makes me cook faster and looser. And when I whip it off to encounter my guests, there is a super-woman feeling, as if I changed from a hidden '50s gal into modern me.

My hip-hop daughter wears a cowl neck, navy blue sweater my mother bought in the sixties on Carnaby Street in London. My father was a foreign correspondent for NBC news and we were posted in London for a time while he flew to hot spots like Algiers for the war of Independence, or Saigon for the insurrections. When my mother bestowed the sweater on Willi she at first bridled at the voluminous neck. She tried to figure out how to cut, tuck, or alter the sweater. It sat dejected in the bottom drawer. Then in a flash of sophomoric wisdom she pulled it out and the cowl cashmere became a staple over cut up jeans, tiny stretch skirts and under jean jackets. Willi says she always feels like smoking when she wears it. It makes sense as my mother's biggest gripe after her stroke was craving and not being allowed a cigarette. Cigarettes had been her touchstone. First Gauloise, then downgrading to Larks; smoke had bathed her for over 60 years. I wondered if perhaps the smell and desire for a smoke had seeped into that sweater.

I see my daughter in her grandmother's extensive sweater collection, I fold the quilts, or rummage in my mother's vintage Chanel and Hermes silk scarves and my hands and eyes remember and honor her. Generations of women woven together through fragile fabric.

GAY IS ONLY A SMALL PART

Why do I have the only messy, toothless, design-impaired gay brother on the planet?

Why don't I have a gay brother infused with fabulousness, instead of one seething with rage, scorn and the intellectual tools needed to inflict horrible pain on all those around him?

I want my brother to have the over-the-top fabulous gene the Queer Eye fellas possess, but instead he's a slob on disability. We, all of us who pay taxes, support his living expenses. You see, my brother claims he cannot help saying whatever leaps into his mind. There is no filter to the destructive, awful things he spies in everyone, and then he disgorges their shortcomings right to their faces. As you can imagine, that pretty much limits his employment possibilities even though he is bright and has flashes of fabulousness flaming out in art. But he would have to be put in an isolation hut, given a camera or paints and forced to slip the work under the door so no one would have to endure the venom that spews forth, scalding mere mortals. It's a difficult life for him, always being right, when *lumpenproletariat* roam the earth looking to ruin his day.

I don't see my brother now, except when protecting my ancient father from him. The last time I encountered Peter – *and can you believe this, his longtime lover is also named Peter? Imagine the lack of levity when you can't laugh at two gay men named Peter living under the same roof. It is either a logo or the nugget for the next reality show. I digress* – the last time I saw my brother was at our parents' house in Durham, North Carolina.

He came down south after a fight with the other Peter. My brother had taken over my father's home and my father called me to come down and get rid of him. It was the sort of call normally made to an exterminator. This was after our mother died.

When she was first sick, I called my brother. My mother confided to me that she often dreamt about hearing a knock at the door and there he was. She adored Peter, but he had not seen her in ten years. I offered to pay for his trip down to see her. I was a mother now and knew how much it hurt when kids were angry or distant. My brother asked if he could have the money instead to make repairs to his house. Peter said, "Call me if mommy gets better, really better or she dies. I am not going down there now."

When we were children, he had been my best friend, my confidant. We used to play with my Ginny dolls, or set up the train set and run over the leg-less or bad haired dolls, making elaborate wrecks where we would swoop in and save them and send them to a makeshift hospital.

We played circus in the living room when our parents were away. We had a secret circus name for our dog, it was Rosebud (and we had never seen Citizen Kane). We gave each other "rockets to the moon." This move necessitated the launcher to be on his or her back with legs tucked in, as if in a deep squat. The one about to go to the moon backed in and rested his or her butt on the waiting feet. The launching sibling then contracted legs and feet and shoved out with a mighty cry, "rocket to the moon!" Often the launchee landed on a lamp or bounced off the picture window. Space exploration can be very dangerous.

My brother also presaged his love for out-of-body

experiences that he later fulfilled with copious drugs. He would beg me to squeeze him and make him pass out. This was achieved by standing behind him while he took massive deep breaths. Then I would cobra my arms around his middle and squeeze until, lo and behold, he would melt in my arms for a few seconds. As I released him, he would revive usually screaming, "Again!" What did we know?

Peter also loved to twirl in circles. I could only last for a few revolutions, but he could go for minutes until he collapsed with the world spinning round him. The best time of year for twirling was Christmas when he would drop under the tree to what he assured me were wonderful whirling rings of light. I never liked drugs, passing out, or spinning. I suppose as the oldest I was trying to be vigilant about a familial reality that seemed to have a genuine preponderance of shift, spin, and a lack of sanity without augmentation.

My father was an alcoholic and my mother, as I only learned when I was 34 and pregnant with my first child, had failed at serial suicide attempts. Her abortive efforts were spun as spur-of-the-moment vacations, meaning she'd go off to the hospital, but the kids would be told she was on vacation. My father's drinking was written off as what newspapermen do, especially those who are sent to war zones. Men will be men and their wives will be crazy.

Aside from the alcoholism, my father suffered from what is now the disease of the moment, intermittent rage disorder. His was more *mittant* than *inter*, but he did have moments of hilarity and wonder that made a child believe halcyon days could be around the corner. Perhaps that is another part of the perniciousness of alcoholism: when the fog of fury lifts, the wonderment returns to the previously poisoned drunk and a soft, imaginative loving person emerges to trick those in their path again and again into believing things could be different.

My father's vengeance was foisted on all of us, but my brother – as the youngest and, I suppose most could have guessed, a gay boy in the fifties household – garnered a whopping share. My father called him Lucy. He really did. He called him Lucy to his face and when others were around. I didn't get it then, but later this offense roiled back on me as an unforgivable imprinting.

My mother was too busy I suppose with her own demons to protect him. She hovered and loved him to the point where, of course, he became branded as a "mama's boy." He sat enraptured while my mother sewed her elaborate creations cloning Paris couture in the Westchester basement. My brother would hoard scraps and do a funny draping thing. His wackiest invention was the "behind guard" fashioned from green shantung silk my father brought back from Hong Kong. Peter cut and knotted scraps and then tied them around his skinny naked body and careened about the house. When we could still laugh together, this was a favorite moment. We could say "Behind Guard" to each other and like members of a secret cult the laughter would roll. Not any more.

The last time I stood face to face with my brother, three years younger but wrinkled, gray and missing too many teeth for his educational level, I was terrified. He pushed me into the wall in my parents' kitchen and spat as he spoke. "I will punch you into dust." He later said it was a metaphor. But I saw the bruises on my father and when I asked if Peter hurt him, my father finally found a way to protect his damaged son. "No, no, I am slow and he just rushed me, that's all."

That was it – I called the sheriff. I had experience with abuse and knew it had to be stopped right away. The first time a woman, or anyone, is abused and you parse the details, making excuses or rationalizing the violence, I believe you make a tacit agreement with your abuser. The first time the aggressor is ALL wrong but after that, some sort of sick pact ensues where the abused dissembles the bad facts and reorders them into an acceptable place. That would not happen again with me.

The cops came and my brother attempted charm saying, "Oh you know, women can be so dramatic." He enlisted my father's help, thinking my dad's misogynistic tendencies might bubble up and side with the boy. Nope. My father told the cops he wanted my brother out. Hell, he wanted me out too; he wanted to be alone, but no one would listen to him. My father said he never wanted to see or hear from my brother again.

My brother sends me angry, ugly postcards. They posit my mendaciousness, my stupidity and they do it in 20-point type so the postal carrier and any neighbors can read it from across the street. Shame is a powerful currency, a legacy passed to children from alcoholic homes and my brother learned shame from a master.

My brother's missives keep arriving at random intervals. I feel sad that he lost the sunny, funny, train crash, behind guard boy, and I also worry about his relationship with my father. So, ever the hero, the oldest child, I approached my father about sharing his address with Peter, or making a phone call. He yelled, "Hell no! I don't want to see or talk to that fucking idiot ever again. Thanks though."

I finally had to ask, "Listen, is this about Peter being gay? Why you won't try to fix things up—" I was about to launch into a spiritual new-agey take on forgiveness and moving forward when my father blustered in.

"— Gay? Gay is a small percent of what your brother is. Asshole is the largest part of who he is. This has nothing to do with gay. It is all about asshole, Ducks." My father rolled over to do what he says he likes to do best, "hug the bed."

In the end, isn't this what we want from a "politically correct" world? Don't we want all people to be treated equally? My father, in his ninth decade, came up with his correlative to Martin Luther King's speech about his hopes for his children:

"I have a dream that my four children will one day live in a nation where they will not be judged by the color of their skin but by the content of their character."

LION QUEEN

What mother hasn't felt like a lioness while rearing babies in whatever jungle she inhabits? A mother is the fiercest beast in the bush, forest, jungle or city. A mother has no ability to make her own needs paramount – she lives, while her cubs are small at least, just for them. I have been that mother lion and even as an aging beast the atavistic instinct to protect my cubs with life and limb remains front and center.

I find it is enlightening to see the universal parent as evinced in other mammals and I had the opportunity to become reacquainted with my leonine role models recently while visiting East Africa. During my *safari* I had the pre-dawn privilege of watching motherhood's fierce muzzle up close, and it let me cherish my own intimate baby time even more vividly.

It was a struggle to wake up every morning in the pitch-black African air. The nights were a cacophony of sounds, squawking bush babies, chattering vervet monkeys, groaning hippos and the endless moaning growls of lions. A lion's call cuts through the night; it can be heard from five miles away, trumping any other beast. Add to these mammalian voices a symphony of insects and amphibians and you envision marvelously wakeful nights. The deep final dark before morning finally found us all fast asleep, no matter how many feet, wings, or gills we had. When the early wake-up knock came, it was hard to fight out of the arms of Morpheus and stumble to find the pot of coffee, inky as the night, left outside my door. I got up before dawn every day for two weeks because at 52, I didn't want to miss a minute in the bush.

When would I return?

I craved the air in the open Land Rover, the expansive geography, the stark Acadia trees, and the hills rolling like God's knuckles on the edge of prairie grass. I charted the wandering movements of the Masai, so shockingly visible because they are swathed in crimson cloth and vibrant plaids all prodigiously piled with beads as they navigate the landscape following and protecting herds of cattle. I was hooked on the pungent smells of baboons, polecats, and elephants, and the delicate fragrance of herbs and flowers. Yet, I was enthralled with the languid lions. They felt like soul mates, more so than the humans with whom I shared this safari.

We had seen a pride on our first morning game ride. The guide spied them on the top of a hill, looking for all my world like an outcropping of maize colored rocks hidden in wavy Serengeti grasses. Then one lioness poked up a nose, her motions echoed by two cubs. The rocks seemed to breathe and the pride awoke except for the most lazy, the male, asleep by himself at the foot of the hill. Females do most of the hunting and the obvious bearing and raising of the cubs, thus lionesses have formed into groups called *crèches* to help raise the cubs.

A *crèche*, like the word in French for a nursery school, is a lion cooperative. The various mothers are all available to nurse or protect any of the cubs, but they try to give the first milk to their own cubs and reject the advances of other hungry cubs until their little ones back off. Lionesses usually have no more than four cubs having only two sets of teats, but most often it is a single or twins so; if milk remains they share.

It takes two years to raise cubs to independence and sadly more than a quarter of all cubs are killed, not by interspecies attackers, but by invading males. Again we see the mother of the species as a victim. It is she who hunts, and she who has to defend against the male. The *crèche* mates will fight together, however male lions are fifty percent larger and often prevail.

I sat wordlessly watching, wrapped in wonder watching these regal creatures. Don't leave, never go back home, never work, never think about anything but these big cats, who fill my peripheral and near vision. After a long time, much shifting of positions in the lion pile, many yawns and stretches, we the human herd moved on out of the now baking sun.

The next morning, we left from Klein's Camp, Tanzania, built by an American in 1929 and still used to stalk prey, not as trophies but as images, or photographs. We rolled down the hills into the Serengeti Game Park, a Tanzanian ranger wearing a tee shirt that shouted in 40-point type, "EAT THE RICH," let us pass into the park.

We careened around the rutted park paths and stopped. Sudden silence filled the open truck. Our guide Mudy, short for Mohammed, was a quiet man with a devilish sense of humor. He told us stories about flying lions, or pretended to hear things to scare us on our walks. He had a rumbling laugh and knew every inch of the Serengeti; this was his land and he reminded us how lucky we were to be visitors. Mudy's silence told us all to pipe down. A gaggle of tourists is about as quiet as a crash of rhinos or a thundering dazzle of zebra, but we heeded Mudy's "HUSH!"

There she was, "the Lion-*ESS*," as Mudy called her. He uttered that name with an emphasis on the final syllable – it gave this mother lion the imprimatur of royalty. This lean, smooth, slinky mother skulked out of the waving, wheat colored grass and onto a small cart road. She ambled a few steps and sat down like a huge, loose-jointed dog. She turned her massive head and uttered a small rumble and her dark-colored, tasseled tail shot up; immediately two lion cubs, about three months old, came scampering. This boy and girl tumbled head over hind with their scrappy tails flapping every which way before they settled at their mother's side.

The lioness sniffed the air and miraculously found us out of range. She scanned the horizon in quiet reverence. She had a large gash on the left side of her neck; this woman was not just at home making curtains, this lioness worked and won. The cubs nuzzled into her belly; I know that sort of caress, a cub who wants nursing. I had suckled, as the guide said, my cubs for a good long time and as a result I carried them, like this mother lion, into many foreign lands safe with the notion that I could feed my offspring and keep them healthy.

I watched as the cubs nestled in and began to nurse in earnest. We could hear the slurping, the gurgling, and happy gulps from our perch in the Land Rover. I loved the sounds of the cubs, but what totally slayed me was the countenance of the Lioness. She sat at first proud, vigilant and then was herself transformed by the act of nursing. Although she remained upright, I saw that wonderful look come over her big, bright face. Her yellow eyes glazed and rolled. Even the fiercest mother is calmed, lulled and nearly sedated while nursing her babies.

I sat in the rear of the Rover and saw myself. Like the lioness I had a boy and a girl who went everywhere with me, they were my babies and hence were at my side at work in the theater from three days old until they trundled off to school. They were my cubs and even now big, tall and wise, I would defend them to the ends of the earth. Even as a middle-aged mother lion I could vividly channel the joy of sinking into a semi-conscious world of nursing mother. I am still both caregiver and vigilant warrior; all parents are.

HEALING / AUGGIE'S ARC

HEALING

Over a year ago I tore the meniscus in my left knee. I believe it was degenerative, but I also must mention that a mere three months before this debacle I joined a gym with the express notion of "getting more giddy-up." Instead, I got much less.

I am stubborn. With less than a modicum of sense, I played too many sports while being coached to the edge of exhaustion and injury. So when a trainer says go for it, I do. But at over 65, this is at my peril. And so I pushed and pushed thinking I might get a bit slimmer, more taut and certainly more mobile. Instead, I tore my meniscus and needed extensive rehab. I could barely walk to the corner or creep up a flight of stairs. I did not want an operation and so my road back was exercise, heat, cold, and electric stimuli, rather than surgery. It took me a fretful year to not see stairs as Everest or to reconsider getting up for a glass of water during a movie at home.

And the entire time I was rehabbing and healing in tiny iterative steps my ancient Maine coon cat was with me. We got Auggie right after September 11, 2001 as a gift for my son, then 12. I felt Henry needed a place where he could pour prodigious affection and take solace from another being. Boys from 12 until… I am not sure since he is 29 and still not snuggly again, seem to become feral creatures and I thought another diffident being might be a comfort. Instead Auggie fell in love with me.

In his dotage he weakened. He lost most of the muscle mass in his left hind leg. The vet said it could have been a stroke, but in truth, modern vets seem to mostly want to do costly tests and keep my creatures overnight. I told the vet as long as it wasn't some progressive, wasting disease, we would both just limp home. And we did.

Auggie has been an inspiration to me. He never bemoans his new less vital status. In his glory days he could leap from the roof of the shed, shimmy along a narrow ledge and arrive outside the second floor bedroom window yowling to be let in at dawn. He still jumps up onto counters and sinks, even though often the attempts are thwarted and he takes a tumble. He is never ashamed and he repeats until he makes it. He must have the strongest shoulders and front legs in cat history, because I see him pull himself up when a leap has left him short.

As an old (or older) woman who had two large babies, I get up to use the bathroom several times a night. And every time, Auggie hauls himself out of bed and walks me to the loo. He stands, waits and returns with me. I always say, "I'm Okay. I can do this alone." But the lovely thing about animals is they ignore you and just remain vigilant. There are never fights like with spouses or children. The same fracas circling around not being listened to, or my strange weirdness at feeling too closely observed, thus my feared incompetence revealed doesn't exist with Auggie. No, with Auggie I am aware this is what he does. I am his person. We go at things together.

I recall a solo sledding trip I took right after I turned 60. I carefully trudged back and forth up the hill packing the snow down with what we used to call a flying saucer, but I believe the Olympic term is "Snow Coaster." It required a few painstaking trips to carve a path. Each time you descend, you go faster and further. Auggie came with me in feather light snow; not to slip, sled and slide, just to observe. Probably to watch over me. He sat on the Adirondack chair and seemed bemused by my human folly. I took more and more runs twirling and bashing into bramble bushes. I fear I may have embarrassed Auggie as I watched him leaving marking his path home with big paw prints. I stayed until the weak winter light dipped behind the barn and the stalwart nuthatches and finches finished gobbling the thistle seeds in the feeder. I felt full of joy. No one was there to see it or share it and still it was palpable and soul soothing. If you sled alone, chortle and return home snow-encrusted at nearly 60, is the ebullience less real because no one saw it save a large feline and feasting feathered friends?

We also used to launch out for long cross-country ski trips. Auggie with his big snowshoe padded feet would often blaze a trail and then circle back to check on me and head out again. I plowed along, glide, kick, glide, kick, bask in the sun, and continue. I now have justifiable trepidations about the idea of falling, or that a brisk, missed kick with what I call my wonky leg would set me back months. I fear an aged, less vital Auggie would exhaust himself trying. Luckily we have a different path we now take in snowy winter.

We slow walk. As soon as I put on boots and wrap up in scarves and sweaters Auggie is sitting by the porch door. We head out deliberately. We both like it better when the snow is fluffy and not frozen on top so we don't slip. I see smart Auggie finding stonewalls to navigate so he keeps a better purchase. We finally make our way to the backfield where an old wooden bench awaits. I brush off the snow, I sit down and he plops onto my lap.

It is here I usually do my meditation. I know, I have been told by teachers that you should not have animals on you, or near you, when you meditate, but I feel we feed each other's calm, so I ignore that instruction. Last week my reverie was broken by what sounded like a small helicopter taking off in the distance. We both swiveled our heads to observe a flock of turkeys lifting up straight into the air and flapping their wings in a racket so loud I swore it was mechanical. We then returned to our quiet introspection.

Today I felt better. I had done my rehab exercises a few days in a row and could see a difference *(why am I so lazy?)*. But I could see Auggie was having a bad time. The recent snow had formed a frozen top layer and although I could sink my chunky self through the snow to gain a better footing, my trusty pal was slipping badly. I thought of picking him up and carrying him, but my instinct was that would hurt his pride.

So I called to him, whistling his tune, "If you're happy and you know it." I whistled into frosty air. I told him I was heading out to the bench and I went picking my way through the less treacherous parts of the backfield. I sat down and soon I saw him carefully navigating his path, treading under the cedar trees where it was mostly melted, over to a log barrier by the lavender patch and finally to me. He leapt up handily and settled onto my lap with paws so cold they telegraphed frigidly through double layers. We sat and looked out. Two old pals watching the world.

I have been unable to look away from the horrible electoral accident that befell my country. I can't stop scrolling, texting, signing petitions, calling politicians, marching, and through it all possessing no belief that any action will bring about change. I feel hopeless in a way I do not recognize. It is a mixture of fear, anger and loss. Out in the backfield I can detach myself from what seems to have become an infectious addiction to Internet, iPad, smartphone and the pernicious world of politics.

Hence the only antidote that seems to assuage this troika of terror in me is nature experienced with a being who seems incapable of being held down by age. Auggie is in thrall only to the fire when we return and a good scratch to his white chin or a rub to his bad haunch. He loves tuna in the ceramic bowl I made especially for him. He cautions me to stop judging and watching everything so closely and he inspires me to inhabit my own less than perfect moment and just be, and purr.

AUGGIE'S ARC

When our Maine coon cat Auggie came to us after September 11th, he was all long legs and enormous, tufty ears like a bobcat. He was born in August, hence the name given to him by my son Henry. Auggie was a gift to Henry, also an August baby, in hopes that he'd be a balm to a new, anxious teenager.

Henry had been at Public School 89 across the street from the Twin Towers on the day they were attacked and fell. I biked to his school, dumped my bike and grabbed up Henry and 11 of his classmates, as I feared the Towers would tip over, right onto his school. My husband told me I was being dramatic and would stir things up if I went to the school. But I am headstrong.

When I arrived the lunchroom was filled with the chatter of hapless middle school kids and terrified teachers. I signed out my son and 11 other kids and we headed home. On my ride over I witnessed people jumping from the high windows and had seen the first Tower collapse straight down, not tip as I imagined. As I got the kids outside I admonished them to not look, to stay together and to run south down the wide sidewalk hugging the West Side Highway.

Of course they looked, just like Lot's wife. And instead of being turned into pillars of salt, they wept. Henry and I had to prod them forward toward our home. I needed him to not fall apart; he was a trooper. We nudged and cajoled crying kids upstairs and into the loft. I ran to the deli and took loaves of bread, cold cuts, milk, cookies and bags of chips. I told the proprietor that if we were all alive tomorrow I'd pay him back. And I ran.

When I arrived back it was chaos. The news had been on the television and kids had seen the hit and Towers falling, over and over. Henry had the presence of mind to herd the kids to the bedroom and put on cartoons. I made sandwiches and tore open bags of chips. I then called my father, a former war correspondent. He told me to fill every container in the house with water and to soak sheets and towels to cover the window crevices with the sopping material to keep out toxic dust. He then asked if I had a friend in Europe. I was to find one, call her, give her the names and phone numbers of the kids. The transatlantic lines are buried under the ocean and hence work very well. She would attempt to reach their parents as our phone lines were going down. The cell phones had already stopped working.

I did as he directed and by suppertime every kid had been returned to their parents and had gone on the long slog home. I defrosted cake with the idea that if I was going to die I wanted to be at "maximum chubby." I put the kids, daughter now 17 and son just turned 13, to bed. Zach and I opened a good bottle of wine and I broke down. Later that night I went out to survey the broken neighborhood. The tanks were rolling up our block and I came home and began to write what became *A Mother's Essays From Ground Zero* and later an opera entitled *Calling*.

The next two months were surreal and we religiously carried out an exercise that we called "Getting to Normal." Henry had seen such horrible, difficult things and I worried about his ability to recover without therapy to which he was beyond recalcitrant. And so I found him Auggie. I suppose we now term them service or comfort animals. But isn't that what good pets have always been? I recall the secrets I told Kimmie, my wirehaired terrier, or Finnegan, the ever-brawling Tomcat. They were my touchstones, ever vigilant, never judging, great listeners and the best cuddlers.

Auggie grew and grew becoming an elegant, and slightly

diffident young cat. Henry seemed to follow the same arc. By the time Henry traipsed off to Saratoga Springs to college he was well over six feet, shaving and muscled. Auggie and I would wait at home. And when Henry visited, it was Auggie he ran to pick up and rub his furry face against. It was Auggie who made late night forays into Henry's room to sleep at the foot of the bed after the tossing and turning had subsided. Henry told me he didn't believe that Auggie slept with him, as he never saw it. But I did. A mother never stops looking in on her sleeping children.

A few years after 9/11 we found a lovely old farmhouse up in the Hudson Valley. With the judicious use of a line of credit on our loft; we purchased the 1799 house and its five acres outright. Our own safe place where we could run away, hide, garden, cook, nap in the sun and perhaps grow very old. We drove up with the cats in tow, Auggie the alpha and then Huey Newton and little Coco.

The cats loved it up there. Mice and tall grass, trees to climb, birds to bother; although I fitted them with bells so the hunt was curtailed. I called them all in at dusk as we had very vocal singing coyotes who nightly announced how closely they hugged our home. We all slept dreaming with the calls of the wild and the Amtrak whistle in our slumber.

Auggie always loved being with me. He sat as I dug in bulbs in fall. Over ten years I had planted about 10,000. I think he was near at hand as each one went into the chilled fall ground. And in spring he followed sniffing the different aromas as I gathered posies for kitchen table bouquets. I took to building stonewalls, to delineate a huge line of peonies I planted. I hauled rocks in from the woods in a cart and Auggie went with me. When the walls were finished I assessed their sturdiness when he'd run along them. If the stones wobbled, I needed to reposition them. And when Henry visited to burn brush or clear trees Auggie came and perched on a bench in order to be near.

As he and I aged, he leapt on my lap more often, or he'd nap on my chest as I lay reading. He was getting lighter and lighter, and eating less. I took him to the vet who proudly pronounced that he had 'old man's disease' and would just waste away. Well, not on my watch. I began to give him heavy cream, I cooked chicken breasts and tidbits of roasts or cans of high-end Bumble Bee tuna and he began to rally. This got him another two years of being a very spoiled old man.

Then his hind legs started to really give out. The new young vet said she thought there were tumors or cysts, but by this time Auggie was 17 and I was 67. I was not going to torture him with an operation. I would keep cooking and pick him up onto the bed or couch.

For Auggie's last Christmas miraculously everyone was together in the country. Auggie was woefully slow and so skinny. But he ate heartily. He tasted moussaka, gobbled filet mignon and lapped his cream. He didn't venture far from the house in the sub-zero temperatures, but he asked to go out and would sit like a proud Centurion watching the snow swirl or the birds grab seed. Henry, now 29, having finished Law School and sworn in as a member of the New York State Bar, sat next to Auggie on the porch steps. He snapped some photos, as Henry put it, when Auggie looked "especially regal with his fur ruffling in the wind."

When we returned to Harlem right after New Year's, Auggie was at his slowest. He was slipping and sliding on the wood floors. He stopped eating the warm roast chicken, and then he even stopped lapping drops of cream from my fingers. I put a yoga mat down for him by the living room couch and for two nights I slept next to him with my hand on his side. I didn't want him to feel alone.

On his last morning he was a quiet, sunken, still furry version of the kitten who came to us. I knew he was on his way out. It was a Friday. I called Henry who was at work and told him he should come if he wanted to say a proper goodbye to Auggie. Henry is a first year attorney and not at liberty to hightail it home for a cat farewell. He kept texting me into the evening; he was stuck at work. I covered Auggie in cashmere as his fur felt so chilly. I lay on the floor next to him and said, "Auggie you have to hold on because Henry is coming. He needs to say goodbye to you."

He waited, his breath so shallow and intermittent. A very old machine slowing carefully to its end. Henry arrived at nearly 9 p.m. I asked if he would like time alone with Auggie. He did. I left and went into the den. 15 minutes later I heard, "Ma, I think he's gone."

I came in and Henry was on the floor with his hand on Auggie. He was stock-still and then our cat took two enormous death rattle breaths, startling both of us. We knew then he was gone. All quiet.

Henry and I stood up and he collapsed into my arms crying. I had not seen this kid cry through the terror of 9/11, the death of grandparents, the crush of his live-in sweetheart leaving him and now here he was a 29-year-old lawyer weeping with his mama over the loss of a cherished longtime companion. I worried that I wouldn't be able to hold him and I was hell-bent that I would not be the first to let go. I willed my wonky legs to be as vigilant as our Auggie would have been. And they held. Henry let go and went to the bar and poured us a glass of scotch. Zachary came in and we three toasted the long, much loved glorious being. To Auggie!

It was still below freezing and I knew we wouldn't be able to drive upstate to bury him. Henry worried I would throw him out in the trash. "NEVER," I told him. I would wrap him carefully and the next day I'd drive upstate and put Auggie in the freezer until spring and a proper burial.

After Henry went home, I chose a towel and curled our kitty's still supple body into a tight ball, similar to his sleeping form. We'd drive back to the country in the morning and deposit him to the extra freezer in the mudroom. In the morning when I came into the living room, Auggie's tufted ears had popped out of the towel, a final poignant greeting. He had after all arrived ears waving.

OWNING BEAUTY

"Imperfection is beauty, madness is genius and it's better to be absolutely ridiculous than absolutely boring."

Marilyn Monroe

THE FRENCH HAVE A NAME FOR IT

Être bien dans sa peau is a French phrase that literally means "to be well in your skin," but it portends so much more.

It means to be at ease or comfortable with yourself. You are physically in fine form but more importantly, you are harmonious with the world. It is a sense emanating from within, and translates to the bubbling, buzzing world outside that this lucky soul is doing well in her skin— *être bien dans sa peau*.

I have noticed that to be really doing well in my skin becomes more and more of a challenge for me and for my women friends, now at the midpoint of our lives. Skin is the body's largest organ, so if we, at life's midpoint, notice changes in our hair, in our metabolism, in our sexuality, imagine what metamorphosis appears daily in our skin. For women in menopause, which happens at different times for every woman—usually somewhere between the 40s and 50s – estrogen levels drop and the skin is no longer as lush as it once was. For men, a life lived with fewer beauty products and lots of sun time, this also translates into aging skin.

We see the manifestations in the mirror, in the shower, or as we gaze at our arms at summer's first warm blush. The change in our skin is glaring and constant. Our skin is changing, drying out, wrinkling, marking, and not bouncing back as it once did. And our endless challenge is to realize how good, how wonderful, and how wise we really are in our skin.

Part of that wonder is the fact that we have been around for a while and jumped other hurdles. We have accumulated wisdom, stood up to bullies, fallen in love, wept, lost family and many of us have actually made family. Each one of these events can give us lines, bumps, scars and life learning. Often when I sit on the old milking stool in my bathroom after a shower, I feel as if I am making a sentimental journey traversing the geography of my body, visiting landmarks as I slather on creams, moisturizers, and lotions. From the tips of my toes, too often shoved into pointed shoes or laced into sneakers to train for the marathon or to traipse across Italian piazzas; I see the signs of time. I see the constellation of veins on the top of my left calf that marks the spot where my son hit a hardline drive that catapulted his Little League team to victory as it marked me for life.

I have a silvery white scar on my right index finger, exactly an inch long that came from a glass that shattered as I washed dishes, the night before leaving on a Caribbean vacation. I stuck a Band-aid on it and got on the plane, but from the way it healed, it obviously should have had a stitch or two. I have a huge scar on my right knee where a taxi sideswiped me and knocked me to the Manhattan pavement as I rode my bike to a photo shoot. It was tended too belatedly and as a result the cut festered and became infected. I have tiny shadow scars from picking at mosquito bites as a kid. These remind me that I haven't gained the ability to leave things well enough alone, and am still prone to pick until I draw blood. I have a scrape scar on my right shin garnered in a swimming pool in upstate New York. I taught my then four-year-old son to swim in this pool and as he took off on his own for the first time, I tripped and banged against the rough concrete steps. I recall my elation at his solo swim tempered with dread as the water around my leg started to turn pink. I was enmeshed in a tempestuous affair that summer, and after it broke off I remember looking at the scab and thinking, "By the time this fades, I will be healed from loving the wrong man." I am lucky that my body has no visible major scars from falls, surgery, or childbirth. I knock on my wooden head as I write this in the hopes I can ward off the evil demons who prey on those who exhibit hubris, the kind of pride I take in my random tiny scars.

I see these scars, along with the freckles, age spots, and wrinkles as a map of myself. My body has a full landscape that is in constant flux and I am trying to embrace it along its journey. These marks in middle age celebrate me as a woman who has lived, laughed, and on occasion languished, yet survived and thrived.

I am not opposed to plastic surgery or dermatological augmentation if in fact it gives people greater self-esteem. But I know it is not for me. I fear it would distract me from that glorious sense of occupying my being, embracing all the mistakes, both psychic and physical, and taking a big dose of learning from them. I am driven to learn. This means I no longer forget sun cream. I know from all the books and my doc friends that there are two major enemies to skin: sun and smoking. But we also know that we can rebuild with moisturizing, drinking lots of water, and even exercising. I care about how I look and feel. I love it when my husband takes my hand or busses my cheek and croons, "Oh baby, you have such soft skin." I'd like him to keep that praise coming for the rest of my life. I didn't always use creams, eschewing them as un-feminist, but now I take my time on the bathroom stool after the shower. I cream up while I am still wet enough to provide moisture for the lotion. I try to apply sunscreen everyday to my face before I venture out on my beloved bike. I get in that shower and use a scrubby and exfoliate to remove the layers of dead dry skin that don't slough off the way they used to. And unfortunately I notice the lines, the crevices, the sags and wrinkles as I smooth on my lotions.

What I try *not* to do is castigate myself and judge my aging face and body. I attempt to see the wisdom of my age and honor it with slathering, touching and loving care. I see value in an older me: I am not provoked as easily, I can organize, call on resources, find connections, and wait for answers, I have an ability to pull threads from the many diverse experiences of my life and weave them together into coherent answers. I have a belief that things will get better. This ability comes *only* with experience, and age. So if I keep gathering information, keep my eyes wide open and my ears ready for the tidbit, I can keep growing, even if my skin slows down.

In other cultures, wise women are revered for all the paths they have walked, often in their leathery skin, but here in America we are committed to a culture of youth that asks everyone – men and women – to attempt agelessness or take a back seat in life. We hear so many women who have entered menopause bemoan the fact that they feel invisible. We feel discarded by our culture, one that wants only the supple, writhing nymphs who populate movies, videos and commercials. These are our norm, so much so that when we see women of a certain age on the screen or even advertising products targeted to middle-aged women we are excited. We long to see ourselves portrayed as we are, chock-a-block full of wisdom, full of scars from falling down and full of pride from getting back up. Our skin is our first line of defense in rebuilding our gumption and our tenacity, so I do like feeling it when I bathe, when I work out, when I make love, when I apply creams, oils, and lotions. I know that how I feel in my skin is more than skin-deep. I know it does trickle down and penetrate my very core.

I long to achieve that highest French praise of being a woman who is doing so very well in my skin, because I know it means I am feeling my age in all the best ways.

FAIR TRADE

"Hey, that's my bike! Don't touch it!" Sometimes I would holler this across the schoolyard as some other kid rooted through the phalanx of bikes that lined the school's entrance. Big blues, or sleek slivers, some with streamers or baseball cards clipped to the spokes. Our bikes were us.

I had a boy's bike. I had to, I was that kind of girl. The cross bar was security and it meant I could tote it on my shoulder for an emergency portage or to show off my strength. My bikes were always blue or black and I never adorned them with stickers or streamers. The seat was round and had curly springs; it felt as if I was riding a tractor when I bounced on the unpaved side roads.

Of course it had balloon tires, fat enough to mash the curb; I could bash stairs or massive potholes and the bike kept rolling. Back pedal breaks were also a must as were no gears. I knew these bikes were old-fashioned, but they were like me. Solid, upright and able to go the distance.

Some girls had skinny bikes with baskets and pink fenders. One of those girls was Peggy Rogers; she would glide over to my house for our nightly summer baseball game. When she carefully dismounted, she didn't swing a wild scabby leg over the seat and drop her bike in a puddle in a mad dash the way I did. No, she parked with deliberate care, even using the kickstand. I rushed everywhere and she seemed perpetually cool.

At that prepubescent moment I was content to be me and I loved my bike. I would never have switched bikes with anyone. There are certain things that can never be traded. I used to think that way about me, about my body. I was always a sturdy stalwart sort. The kind who doesn't get sick even if you leave her out in the rain. Not a wisp of a creature who gets hurt in tumbles or breaks if she hits the ball too hard.

Peggy Rogers was at bat. We were in third grade. She was a lousy player, but she had blond hair and it was wound into lustrous, long banana curls. These were formidable baubles for a nine-year-old to brandish and I felt dowdy sporting my burnished brown, boy-bob. Peggy held the bat in a very contorted fashion and yet somehow managed to get a hit now and again.

This time however, when she hit the ball she cracked her wrist. We all heard it and I wanted to yell out, "if you held the damn bat the way you are supposed to, this would have never happened." You aren't supposed to criticize someone, even a dip, when she breaks her wrist. Peggy watched all the games that summer from the grassy bank. Her hair perfect and the sun streaming behind her imbuing her a vague phosphorescence. She was a striking, placid opposite to me.

And although she fascinated me, I didn't want to be her. I didn't want to trade my bike, my being for hers. We went separate directions. I went to college and she stayed and married some man who I always thought was dull. She would ask me to say things to her in French or tell her about classes and books; sitting in her perfect kitchen drinking tea and laughing about when we used to ride through the neighborhood. I realized it was she who wanted to be me.

I grew up and live in a world tainted by Madison Avenue where a woman can never be too thin, too blond, or too rich. I would never belong to that troika. In my early forties I had a friend, a socialite, who was beautiful. Her hair was like liquid silk somewhere between the color of gold and carrots. She was a fluid walker and wore the tiniest black dresses. Her wallet was full of money and she never had to hustle for a babysitter because her big townhouse had one living right there at her beck and call.

When she left her husband she needed someone to take to some of the best parties in NYC and for a while, I was the one in the back seat of the limo. There were cocktail parties with martinis and dinner parties with tiny portions and tinkling glasses. This woman always bitched about what she should wear, but I had only one great black dress purchased in Paris earlier.

One night, on the way to some event she looked at me imperiously pushing aside her blond cascade and remarked, "You always wear the same thing."

"Yeah I know, it's my only dress, so what?"

"Well, when we go to parties, I have noticed that at first all the men want to talk to me, but then as the night goes on they all want to sit with you. You know it's because you have words and you are funny. You have *stories*!"

She hissed the last part as if I had taken some unfair advantage of a situation by having the audacity to tell tales as opposed to wear designer clothes and starve myself.

I know stories and robust health are great, but there are moments when they are no match for the holy trinity of blond, thin, and rich. So I try to love my solid robustness. I marvel at my strength when splitting logs or rowing a crew race. I still love the muscles that lurk even in middle age. But I have missed being the American ideal. There will always be some spectral creature waiting in the wings to shatter my palpable presence and reduce me to the hulking lummox who lurks in my soul.

I look at those women on movie screens and in the supermarkets, their arms and legs flow from their fragile cores.

And I turn to assess my core, my essence – would I trade it? My body has not yet betrayed me. I still ride my bike through New York City winters, rain, snow, and sleet to work or black tie. I take care of friends with the flu and rarely get sick. I eat cookies off the floor and drink the water anywhere.

I still like to dance all night and stayed up 'till 4:30 am for my daughter's 21st birthday then got up the next morning to make breakfast for stragglers. I don't know why I have been blessed with this strong core, but I have. And yet every plus has a minus.

When I am out in the world I review other women. The women who men and the world admire as ravishing. The ones who will be cherished and held and protected so they won't taper and dwindle. I find I'm not one of them.

I am drawn to pictures, to the commercials, and to the real-life women who look as if they stepped out of Vogue or an Armani ad. I think from time to time that I might trade. I would yell across a bike-littered Central Park, "Hey, I will trade you my big bike for your 12-speed racer. Oh, it comes with this body. Okay, I know it isn't trendy, but it doesn't usually break down; it can work real hard, and seems resistant to wrinkles." I would mount my new bike with its spidery thin tires and curved handlebars propelled by the new me: a long sleek, aloof blond.

Every time I think of trading this way I am appalled. I pull myself into a corner of the garage and take a hard look at that solid cycle leaning against the wall. That bike is me: dents, wiggly spokes, endless adventures, and a basket full of goodies.

"Never-mind. I don't want to trade bikes," I would scream across the field of Central Park. "Nope, not even if you toss in some neon shorts and toe clips. This bike stays with me, thanks!"

BLONDE AND BOOZY

I had colored my hair since I was 42, the same year, the same moment I left the father of my children. It was a brutal relationship and he was a creep, but in truth, by the end, I was not much better. I suppose I wanted to regain some of the years I lost staying in such a *dysfunctional* (does that mean the same thing in polite company as "really fucked up?") relationship. I lost much of my belief in humanity and myself during the 15 years I was with him, and of course it was foolish to ponder that more youthful hair might be restorative. But I am and always will be a magical thinker.

At first I had my hair professionally done, but that was expensive, money I didn't have, but I convinced myself that since I wore it every day, it was a good value. Then as we got poorer and my daughter got older, she offered to do it for me. So my live-in teenage hairdresser and I had dates in the bathroom every six weeks and we played "Marlena," the name she had taken when she played make-believe hairdresser back in preschool.

Later, Willi went off to college and I tried to schedule hair appointments with her before holidays, but the silver, the gray, the light hairs were on a march and seemed to be back before three weeks were up. And so I took to doing my hair myself with no mirror to see the back, lots of splashing of color on the tile floor, and occasionally big missed patches. Willi would fill in the blanks when she came home.

When I was 63, I went on a trip to Africa to observe first-hand a passion project I had been working on. I colored my hair before leaving, not to look good in the bush mind you, but by now it had become a ritual. Cover the silver before a trip, a party, a speaking engagement. Cover, dye, or conceal something about me that was becoming so vital that it announced itself with a greater and greater vigor every week. Ageing brings a diminution of many things, physical prowess, memory, willpower and wait, did I forget, did I say memory? So it was amazing to see that my hair, my shiny, silver hair seemed to be growing at a prodigious rate.

There was no hair washing on my trip and definitely no ability to dye my hair during the month I was away. The African sun has the power to bleach everything it touches. And so, as I worked and sweated my hair began to reveal a bright silver racing stripe down the middle of my head. I didn't have a mirror for weeks, but people took pictures and I saw that I was changing from a deeply entrenched brunette to a silvery vision who glinted in the glare.

When I came back, I made the decision to stop dying my hair. I would let it be natural: in some places silver, in others salt and pepper. Whatever it wanted. Summer seemed the perfect moment. I could ride my bike, swim, play tennis, walk all over the place with no hat, no protection for my hair and just let the sun at it. I would wrench it back into a ponytail or bun and by the end of summer; by my mid-September birthday, I would cut off the brown and welcome a full head of silver.

One day in early summer I went to meet my daughter for a drink in a downtown bar before we went to the theater. I am a light drinker, but as I have gotten older I can drink a glass and a half of wine. This is a big step. My son still calls me "One and Done." But here I was ensconced in a bar with a proper cocktail set out in front of me with my silvery halo surrounding me. My daughter walked right by me. I called out to her, she blurted, "How was I to know you? Look, you are blond and boozy!" We laughed so much and decided that was how I should chase the rest of the summer, hell, maybe the rest of my life. Better than dark and abstemious, which seemed my moniker up until now.

I am loving the silver hair. Of course my cool daughter emailed me from the South of France with the news blast that two-toned hair was all the rage and called *ombre,* meaning "shadow" in French. I had two very distinct tones of hair and some sun kissed highlights. But the silver was amazing and soft like baby's hair. Men were flirting with me. Some really old men, meaning my cohorts, but young men as well. "I love your hair, how did you do that?" one ultra-tall, blond, ice blue eyed wanna-be model asked me, as we sat waiting for separate meetings at a magazine. "I didn't do anything. I stopped coloring it; it's natural at this point." Incredulous, he told me I should figure out how to do it and offer it to others. "You're sweet," I said, but I thought, "YOU ARE DELUSIONAL." Then cute men kept complimenting me. I tried to brush it off as just a perk of oldness and then they would go full court press to "You're not old!" So now I just say thank you, as I really do not want to be disingenuous, but heck, it feels good to get a compliment from anyone at this point.

I don't regret coloring my hair for 20 years. I have been with my wonderful husband for nearly that long and he is seven years younger than I am, and one of those wildly handsome men who get better looking every year, an unfair advantage that I thought might be mitigated with my dark brown hair. But now I know that what I bring to my life really is evinced in this wonderful new mane of silver hair. No one, no matter how creative or adroit with the color brush and a palate of dozens of colors, could ever have created the sprockets of pitch black, chestnut brown, colorless white and the sheen and shine of real sterling silver. I love it. I just can't recognize that it is me. But how exciting that at nearing 65 I can be an entirely new person, one that my own daughter will zoom by in a dimly lit bar. Blond and Boozy here to stay.

OUR WALLS

I have five acres in the Hudson Valley, an old farm with a house built in 1799 and a barn from 1840. I know the house's age from the deed and the barn has wonderful graffiti from, as I imagine it, the boys and men who raised it. "HGS 1840" is scratched high in the haymow.

The woods surrounding the property are dotted with tumbled down stonewalls – the remnants of farmers clearing land to make ready for planting. I have cleared a path to the closest wall and have been hauling it out stone by stone. I am bringing the stones out into the light to reconstruct a wall, which I hope will run the length of my peony plants.

A well-moneyed acquaintance, asked why I didn't just get a pallet of stones, better yet, a few pallets and a few men to build the wall. "You know you could have that done in a weekend." I relish that I have hidden my lack of deep pockets from some of the folks in my circle. I often wear my heart, my past, and my balance sheet on my sleeve when I should be more circumspect.

I told old moneybags that I loved going into the woods and picking over the stones. And I do, but I would have told her that even if it weren't true. Or by telling her, do I make it true? A rabbit hole of logic. I also told her that the new pallet of stones are burnished and clean and don't have the patina of age that I lust after. New stone lacks the amazing moss and rich, dusty lichen in orange and pale seafoam.

As I was extolling the wonders of these stones where the growth, chips, mottled colors and errant cracks create a patchwork of beauty, I was stopped dead in my tracks. That is *me*. I am a sturdy stonewall made of aged granite and mica.

Look at my face, the sunspots, the freckles, the scar under my chin, and the lines around my mouth. And this is only the top stone. The marks come from tears, fear, sunshine and laughter, climbing too recklessly and falling too hard.

When I was a theater producer, I commissioned a wonderful dance piece with the consummate choreographer Bill T. Jones. The work was called *Perfect Courage* and in it the more-than-perfect specimen that is Bill T. carefully undressed. He kept the audience rapt telling the story of every scar on his body: the midnight swim, the tussle with a brother, the chicken pox, the knife fight in the kitchen and on and on, until he was as near to naked as polite theater would allow. He stood in a dance belt with his arms akimbo and pronounced that this was the geography of his life. He was as complicated as any relief map, mountains, rivers, streams and desert. Yes, complicated, I thought, but predominantly perfect in a way that only a few human beings will ever achieve.

And so it is with my wobbly walls, which now outline a peony path of 96 plants that burst forth during a six-week period every summer. I know every stone: the duck, the tables, the snail, and the mini Stonehenge. I know the colors when washed and gleaming, gray-blue, pink, obsidian, flaky rust and on and on. I touched each stone at least twice. Once when found in the woods, again when placing it in the wall, and sometimes additionally to repurpose it if my cat assistants showed me it couldn't withstand a feline walk.

My skin is the same - a wall that surrounds and protects me from the thorns of the garden and life. My mother used to say to us when we were hurt by words or deeds, "Duck's back kids, duck's back." She meant that you had to have a tough, water repellent exterior to get through the wayward, thorny paths of life.

SIGHT BEYOND EYES

I've been grocery shopping without my glasses. And I've been known to read the stock pages with the newspaper flat on the floor, while I perch high up on a chair. Have I bought ricotta cheese thinking it's low-fat yogurt? Do my teenagers stand on chairs and imitate me? Of course!

This whole eyesight thing has caused me, on an afternoon or two, to dreamily ponder the pagan goddesses— the crones of old who might lose their sight, but were considered visionaries. I can't see *them* wearing glasses.

I don't willfully shop without glasses. I forget them in part because I see well at a distance. I wear glasses for reading, but in the grocery store there are so many other messages conveying what the product is, I almost feel reading is superfluous. If some other enterprising cereal company comes up with a bright yellow box and red letters, then, kids bring home that new big box. And as for Parmesan cheese versus Romano, well it's a toss- up anyway. They better not be selling anthrax or cocaine in those plastic tubs because to me it is all the same.

Without glasses shopping is an adventure. The meat doesn't just look raw; it looks vibrant and fresh. There are no spots on the apples, and if there are spots I will turn them into applesauce when I get home. And I rarely look at the prices. I have wandered into the kitchen wearing my reading glasses and wonder who could have bought the twelve-dollar vermouth-soaked olives. Then I recall how my husband praised the martinis I made with them. So I told him that farsightedness was the mother of marvelous martinis. He loved that.

The kids are still hollering from the other room, "Hey Ma, I love these new English muffins, they have raisins in them!"

"Oh lovies, I thought you'd like them."

Sometimes the mistakes are really culinary treats, but other times I'll hear, "These are no *fat* Triscuits, they really should say no *taste*. Ma, you have to wear your glasses when you shop!"

"Shop for your own fuckin' groceries," I want to say, like a foul-mouthed salty almost-grandmother. But they've asked me to curtail my swearing. So instead of profanity I inquire if they can find *anything* worth eating in the $300 worth of food I just bought. You have to be tough to be a menopausal mom with teenage kids. No time for reverie about goddesses and magic. Just when they are at their most petulant, edgy and hormonal, so are you. Really, toughness isn't the issue – flexibility and humor can be the salve that turns frustration and anger into useful insight.

Maybe dimming sight open doors to unseen adventures. I've always been on top of every detail, perhaps a little too in micro-management for my family's taste. Now I get to be looser around the edges. Not seeing certain details adds a little mystery and fun into the mix.

Without glasses, with softened sight, even the details of my changing self, the lines announcing old age, are hazy and distant. My dimming eyesight helps me to see the marks of time with no edginess, like the time of day when the light makes everything blend into violet, not yet gray.

There's something about not being able to see all the damn details that makes life a little more fabulous and eccentric. It is, a whole new perspective.

I am a woman usually content with the augmented wisdom or spiritual milestones that occur as time proceeds. I have always had a kind of feminist pride since I was one of the early women at Yale Business School, when we were not so much thought of as equals, but rather as cute accessories. My mother was a product of an original crucible of feminism—the Seven Sisters schools. She went to Wellesley and believed that women ruled the world; they just didn't have the heart to tell the men. My mother and I read Betty Friedan, who I was told went to Smith College, but we shouldn't hold that against her. We also read Gloria Steinem, and I was admonished not to hold her blond tresses against her. My mother was a funny feminist. She believed in a wonderful combo of style and women's rights. With this indoctrination, I believed I would be okay with growing older. My mother taught me that women who implanted youth surgically were superficial because they didn't embrace reality.

I have always attempted to subscribe to that belief. That was until a recent trip to Hawaii. In the hotel bathroom there was a mirror and worse, one of those magnifying mirrors with mini klieg lights. Looking in it, I saw every expanding pore, new wrinkle, and errant hair. I saw cute freckles turning into age spots; all enlarged times 10. I was flabbergasted. This was not a fabulous adventure. In fact, it hit me: I am no longer young.

Those mirrors should be banned, and nobody should have to pluck or wax their eyebrows, ever. They call them "beauty mirrors." Why? All I could see were flaws: there were lines beginning around my lips (and I have never smoked!). The discoloration on my cheeks from too many years of unprotected fun in the sun was appalling. All that time spent biking, swimming, running and falling in the grass with nothing (certainly not an SPF 15) between the air and me but sweat had taken its toll. The skin around my eyes now had the quality my mother used to call "crêpey"— as in the party decoration paper favored in the fifties with a kind of thick transparency to it. Crêpey was always a negative in her parlance, as was someone who was "long in the tooth."

My mother instilled in me a bit of judgment on women who try to look young when they are no longer. She always hated the false behavior of women who comported themselves in a manner she termed "too gamine" for their age. My mother knew style. She wore Chanel suits, either real ones bought in Paris or her own knockoffs whipped up in her sewing room. She had carnelian lips and smelled of Norell perfume and Lark cigarettes. Coming from a place of her own deep and substantive style, she pooh-poohed hair too long and clothes too tight or revealing on women of a certain age— beyond childbearing.

"No one," she used to say, "certainly no man, wants to look at a wrinkled décolletage." My mother and I are different. At this point in my life I have the feeling that a little flaunting is a good thing, in fact, it's safe in a brand new way. Yes, my décolletage is changing, but still I insist on a hint of lace peeking out of my husband's borrowed Brooks Brothers shirt that I often wear over tight jeans.

I firmly believe spiritual strength should offer us our own sense of confident beauty despite the physical changes. Or do I? That chance encounter with the mirror in Hawaii was the first time I saw the indisputable appearance of *the crone:* the woman of legend and myth who is revered for her wisdom, not her youthful body. The difficulty lay in the fact that she had begun to appear on my face, before I was ready for her psychologically. She was hurrying me to get right with the physical changes. Because let's face it, I still felt like I looked seventeen, well, at least like a woman in her thirties.

I came home from the Hawaiian trip and looked at photos of myself when I was younger; leaning on a pony in

Wyoming, or resting my elbow on my thigh at the Spoleto Festival in Italy. I saw that a gorgeous young woman whom I knew (because she was me) had been out of sync with herself. I had so doubted my gifts, my value, and my abilities because I was never the traditional treasured beauty. I was dark, I was not thin, and I was always a mouthy tomboy. I was raised to believe that "pretty is as pretty does." I remembered thinking that if I was not pretty, I was going to "do": be bright, do good works, get a big education, cook, think, read, offer things to others. How tragic, when today I look at those photos and think as I do about my daughter, "God, what a vital beauty!" I can reflect back on being adored by strings of men and usually having a lover, but I felt always it was not my beauty that drew them but the fact that I was a "good sport." When I look back, I see the curves, the long shiny wall of hair, the flashing eyes, flawless skin, and I think: "I missed it. I missed the moment."

In short, once again, I find I am in jeopardy of "missing it." I have had such trouble viewing myself with kindness—because I am, after all, still in my own body and I can feel a loss of the immediate tone that we all sigh at in young women. They all seem like vigorous rubber bands, while I feel held together by a less resistant tug.

Now I've reached this in-between place, the one called by some cultures "woman between winds" a woman who is no longer blown over by the occurrences of nature. She stands solid before any storm, like an aged tree. Part of her solidity, her rootedness, comes from a sense of self. I see that in youth, I ignored the truth of my body and now in aging, my heart is ignoring the truths of my wisdom. With this revelation, I promise not to make the same mistaken judgment about myself twice.

How divinely ordained it is that our eyesight diminishes first, because it is with the inability to inspect myself up close that I can overlook my unfamiliar self. With less focus on my external self, I can turn my gaze inward.

When I embrace the slightly out of focus edges I feel less angry, less frustrated, happier and more hopeful. With this softened vision, lines, marks and the hostilities of time melt away. Not just on me, but also on everyone I see. When my adolescent kids bemoan their pimples and imperfections all I can think is "this is a canvas of unmarred beauty." When my husband talks about the gray in his beard, to me it appears he has a distinguished square chin made softer by a few glowing highlights.

I think for now, despite the fact that I have about four pairs of glasses tucked in "don't forget them" places, I will continue to not wear them and pursue my intrepid shopping adventures. And I vow, I will never, ever get one of those "beauty" mirrors. What would I gain? Clarity? Well that's all relative. What I have is surprise, softness and a sense of forgiveness—maybe even insight. My eyes may be dimming, but my insight and intuition are deepening.

FABULOUS FIFTIES

The fifties have become a treasured era. Everything from finned cars to early rock and kitschy appliances are in vogue. Everything is cool about the fifties except being born in the fifties. That decade marks you as an elder.

Now 55, I started to write this as a complaint about the endless work and attention needed to be over fifty. I am finding it takes a huge amount of time if I devote myself to the minutia of being middle-aged.

I should meditate, do aerobics, Pilates, and lift weights. I need to combat my creeping inflexibility, my spreading chubbiness, and if I watch the commercials correctly, my crumbling bones. Then there is the nutritional piece. I need to eat more healthfully. That means I can't gulp food while typing, talking, folding laundry or doing a host of other things. I observe that the slimmer folks actually eat with a calm relish rather than a canine craving to consume. So even middle-aged eating has to take longer. And I shouldn't grab a sandwich, because we all know that bread is the devil. So I have to fix a salad or vegetable stew. All of this is eats up my day.

I have to remember to take vitamins and calcium, remember the crumbling bones. I have never done this before. I was a healthy, big girl who felt I took in more than my share of nutrients. Now when I walk past the medicine cabinet it, too, upbraids me for something I haven't done. I have added vitamins to my ever-expanding list.

I have to meet deadlines and develop new work sources simultaneously; all to pay tuition at Columbia, the tennis coach, and a portion of my ninety-year-old father's new assisted living. So often I am swimming to red ink while doing all these other tasks. I would like to practice my cello, but instead it chides me with its curvy shape and silent strings. I want to play it for the wonder, but also because decoding difficult information keeps my brain from atrophying further.

In that same vein, I try and practice my languages. I'd like to learn chess, I make passing attempts to scribble in my journal and take a pottery class. Sometimes I am doing this because I love it, but on occasion I feel as if my life were attacking me with everything I am not doing. I want to volunteer and visit friends, send emails, and to talk about girl stuff.

I have deadlines and meetings, and when I return home the cats scurry up to me joyfully and I see they need brushing. They don't seem to care, but I know my husband's allergies would be well served and the kitties wouldn't have hair balls or mats; but it is all my fault for not being better organized or more motivated.

I am even resentful of my teeth, which need brushing twice a day – that is a lot of attention for things that mostly get me into trouble by eating too much anyway. And what about older skin? I now know that middle-aged women need to exfoliate on a regular basis. As we age it seems our skin just doesn't slough off every few days like back in the vigorous days. So now I have this product that sits in the bathroom and says, "USE ME."

Quotidian chores require attention – like dry cleaning, laundry, hand wash: that was yesterday. Vacuuming, toilets, and any flowers that might make home life more fabulous. Sometimes I am even mad at the dwindling posies as they mean I have to empty, wash and reconsider spending on such ephemeral niceties.

When do I find time to vegetate on the couch cradled by the fuzzy cats, wrapped in a blanket (that probably needs to be hand-washed) and just read a book? Not anything I am supposed to read, but a novel, a memoir, a mystery. Sometimes even then I ruminate that my reading time would be better spent reading spiritual texts, or "eat healthy" books, you know, those kinds of books that make you feel righteous.

As I wind up my whine about everything it takes to maintain my life in the fifties, I had a vision. I see the Via Nacional in Havana, Cuba on a Saturday night. I see a parade of fifties American cars in varying stages from glorious renovation to dilapidation, just like many of us fifties babies. I remember riding in gypsy cabs on hot Havana nights, and I recall the conversations I had with the drivers who were also the cars' mechanics and virtual lovers. None of the owners of the Chevys, Caddies, Dodges, or Fords bemoaned the upkeep of these vintage beauties. It was something they did. They had to oil the leather, be creative in replacing parts and take care to clean, polish and cherish their charges. They couldn't run these cars at full throttle past the roaring sea on the *Malecon* anymore, but those venerable vintage babies still turn heads with class and vintage panache.

And in a flash, I saw myself. I glimpsed my vintage self who needs exfoliating and dental whitening, hair color, workouts and attention to nutrition. I know I can't move the way I used to, or ride the wildest ponies, but I am still a keeper. I am not interested in real bodywork to nip and tuck and erase my rusty spots, but I can give myself regular tune-ups at the gym and give myself better diet light on sugar and alcohol.

I am doing a little renovation, reclaiming my ascendance as a member of an incredible era. I have vintage memories and the requisite knowledge that comes with living fully for over five decades.

WHAT IS THIS THING CALLED LOVE?

"The wound is the place where the light enters you."

Rumi

THE MIND'S GARDEN
HOARDING HURT

When I was in college I tripped over the first love of my life. Bobby was a boy who became a man before my eyes and we wandered into the adult realm of sex, drugs, rock and roll, foreign films, and tiny apartments. We lived together and I treated him less well than he deserved.

He was smitten with me and, although I adored him, I loved more what he unleashed in me. So when the opportunity came to have a grown-up affair with my former high school art teacher, I leapt at it. And since it was the late '60s, I believed I had to tell my sweet Bobby about it. After all, weren't we supposed to celebrate this newfound equality, men and women standing toe-to-toe for feminism, rallying behind the pill and politics?

I also told him in a matter-of-fact way about the subsequent affair I had had with the twice-my-age, married manager of the restaurant where I worked. This man had flipped me upside down, spun me around and then returned to his wife. And so, after the summer between my freshman and sophomore years, I was left emotionally slack-jawed but equipped with sexual vocabulary and a salacious travelogue that short-circuited any prospect of settling down with someone my own age.

And yet I returned to the tiny apartment Bobby and I shared; squishing into our single bed, making hallucinogenic spaghetti sauce for our friends, and enjoying our sloppy sheep dog. But I was no longer in love with Bobby, and he knew that.

We stayed together for another six months, during which I was unfaithful, but joyful whenever we found ourselves together. Bobby became morose and distant; he had every reason to feel that way. Finally I moved out, right into another boy's apartment just down the street.

I am not proud of this behavior. I thought I was being modern, off the cuff, sexually liberated, but I thought too much about myself, and not enough about the detritus I left behind.

What I am proud of is that Bobby and I have maintained a friendship for five decades that dims and flares with varying intensity, but endured. He is Bob now, a middle-aged man who races and restores cars; a former pre-med student who turned his desire to care and cure into a thriving business restoring classic beauties.

This past fall I crept back into regular touch with Bob when I was searching for a car as a gift for my husband's 50th birthday. By chance, Bob had just restored a 1976 MGB and it was exactly what my man wanted. I test-drove the car with my 17-year-old son. Bob helped get it inspected; he pointed me to classic-car insurance and special plates that read "ZINC 50," my husband's business and his age. We were back and forth on the phone often, Bob and I, and I visited his shop.

On the day I picked up the MGB – after he had given me a mini tutorial in non-automatic chokes, the hidden latches for trunk, bonnet and glove box— Bob took a breath and said,

"I had a nightmare about you."

I wanted to know; so he went on.

"We were back in college and you were having that

affair with that restaurant guy, Peter, right? It was the same thing all over again. You leaving me, me feeling hurt, and angry that I hadn't stood up for myself enough."

I went to him and said how sorry I was for everything. I had apologized for the damage over and over in the past.

"Hey, don't get me wrong," said Bob. "I love my wife, I love my daughter, I am not sitting here with a hard-on for you; I am as confused by this as you are. I just think it's crazy the way brains keep things stored up, like some sort of dormant garden – and then maybe by seeing you again, it's as if I kicked over a rock and out crept all this hurt."

We talked more, laughed, hugged, and I roared off in the MGB. The autumn leaves swirled at the tires, the wind felt more pronounced, and the car squealed on the curves. As I waited for the light to change I started to cry. The sun was setting early now and the chill air stung me when I rolled down the window and let in the September melancholy.

Where does all of this come from? All these emotions we warehouse over years, over decades? We change calendars, celebrate milestones, but the gardens of our minds hoard sadness, hurt and disappointment. We can't predict or avoid what will release these dormant demons. We just have to acknowledge they exist, honor them as part of our past and keep on with life. The only defense I know is joy and forward motion.

MIDDLE AGE SEX: NOT THE MIDDLE OF THE ROAD

Some writers, scribbling, musing on aging, on life and perspectives, espouse a belief that no one wants to read an upbeat book on getting old. They are sick, they say, of aphorisms and plaudits extolling sagacity over sagging. And I get their point. But suppose we acknowledge that yes, we are closer to the end of the ride; yes, we are creaking, aching and sagging in spots. And yes, we are sometimes or often confused. After acknowledging the downsides, can we then explore and revel in the wisdom or perspectives that age brings? And here's a surprise, what about the orgasms?

Am I the only one who has these earth shaking middle-aged orgasmic episodes? Crazy comings where I think, not only will my city dwelling neighbors hear me, but hell, what will they think when the walls have tumbled into the street and I have to fess up to the emergency workers who have once again rushed to my oft-beleaguered downtown neighborhood? "Oh sorry, it was just us," I say sheepishly as my husband stands by blushing.

Or what happens if the house falls down when I have been at it by myself? Allowing an aging me to pretend time is a mere construct of some frizzy haired physicist as I travel to when I was 19, or experience lovers from different epochs simultaneously and never have to talk or explain, only revels in my amassed knowledge. Then when the firefighters ask, "Did your husband get out okay this time?" I will have to look at them and grin saying, "I have only myself to blame." Oh, I can continue the fantasy as I offer New York's Bravest a safe, sexy haven, if they ever find themselves in my neighborhood again. "Just buzz the door where the walls wiggle," I'll say grinning over my shoulder.

I don't want to sugarcoat this, my fabulous sex is not frequent, but it is mind-bending, consciousness-expanding and long-lasting. What I find is that my middle age, hormonal diminution has taken the edge off my desire, but hell, I almost welcome that. My sex — let me be brutal – my over-the-top sex drive, got me into a passel of trouble. Do I have to enumerate? Okay, my most egregious, most oft-made misstep is that I mistook lust for love. Hell, I had two children, the best kids ever, with a man with whom I could not converse or share a spiritual moment. But we had a run of wild sex. We ran away from work and met for sex, we missed planes fucking on the bathroom floor, and we stood watching the seals in Central Park and did it in my office. That was over thirty years ago, so the Parks Department can't prosecute me for contract violations, right? But this man did the same thing with other women. He had sex with one of my friends while she stayed with us, and I slept in our bedroom. I was aware of this and to my discredit, I stayed.

My sexuality gave me a terrible blindness. Or perhaps my symptoms of neediness, father issues, low self-esteem or whatever other momentary malady prevailed, caused me to act out with an unbridled sexuality. When I made a commitment to be married and love, trust and honor one man, Zachary, who I knew would reciprocate, it hit me with a thud of fullness and joy.

Sometimes I don't reflect my love and joy to my husband because I complain about needing more sex, wilder sex, more frequent, more experimental, more, more, more whatever. And he as ever, well, he listens and loves me. But lately I complain less and appreciate more. When I suggest long baths and loving sex to follow, I know he is relieved I don't want to go to the roof or do it on an airplane, and somehow our current sexuality is so much more. He is a super-loving, loyal, generous husband and father, and he has coaxed those characteristics out in me along with earthshaking orgasms.

I do still have my crazy, private time where all the men, women or imaginary beings in the universe can roam free, giving me pleasure and rain down a host of stimulation. My busy brain and body are content to have both, as I continue to appreciate, or try to like the me outside the saggy neck, chubby tummy or spotted hands. Somehow I attempt to see my energy as infinitely expanding. It takes me on trips where the body and the creaky knees are just so much wallpaper. The real beauty is my vibrating core— and that is quite a trip.

MONOGAMY
44 YEARS ON THE SAME BIKE

I have had a four-decade monogamous relationship with a true love. My bike.

When I started riding my three-speed after college graduation in 1972, I never thought to bank the money I saved every day. Instead I began buying fresh flowers. I intuited the money saved on transportation was my extra cash because I biked everywhere. Now 44 years later I am still on my bike. It is one of the great loves of my life.

I have ridden home from work twice in labor. I honestly could not have considered lumbering into a cab with someone I didn't know, gasping and occasionally screaming. However peddling home in labor from La MaMa, on East Fourth Street where I was the Executive Director, to my loft in TriBeCa seemed like the logical choice. I rode home first in December for my daughter, and again in August three and a half years later, for my son. I stopped pedaling along the way, gagged and groaned and made my way home; and I would do it again.

On my bike I feel powerful, safe, silly and thrifty. What an extraordinary combination. If packaged and advertised on TV, this amalgam would surely sell soap, cereal or beauty products. My bike is a lifestyle, a true love affair. I know on occasion I come off as a zealot, or a proselytizer, but to me it's clear. A bike is near to free, and even when it is stolen, you can amortize the cost of a new one in a matter of weeks if you are a public transportation commuter. And if you are prone to cabs, the bike pays for itself in days. I am talking regular, simple cheap bikes, not designer, fifty-speed mountain bikes. My bike is reminiscent of childhood. I get on, balance and pedal off. You repeat until you arrive at your destination. I get to understand the pitch and throw of the land. I notice the first spring and the fog off the river. I observe rush hour, but don't really participate as a bike can slip through and sally forth taking me home. And my bike, equipped with a huge "news boy" basket will schlep all my parcels home without lugging.

Bikes are good for the world, we now say they are green and in fact mine is British racing green. Bikes are good for you. Even though I am chubby, or BMI challenged (I think of myself as a full-fat cheese), my doctor still annually extols the value of my bike. "Wow, low blood pressure, the kidneys, lungs, and liver of a 20-year-old, that bike is good to you!" I may have to give a nod to genes as my equally rotund father smoked, drank, and yet lived to 92. So I'm counting on genetics and biking to provide maximum health benefits.

Biking provides an innate sense of freedom. The air cocoons me on a summer's night as I head home whilst others wade into humid subways or haggle for cabs. It provides a magnificent sense of power for me as an aging woman. I never worry about how I will get home from any event and I am faster than most other conveyances. I careen from the east side to west in a jiffy. I can do three art openings from Chelsea to SOHO and back in the time others say "Taxi!" And my transportation is fun.

I feel like a kid on my bike. My legs pedal or I let them dangle when I take the long hills home. I know the hills, the badly paved streets, the good ice cream stops or soup places, the fruit vendors with plump cherries and ripe pineapples. Plop, it all goes into the basket and I carry on.

My bike also allows me to observe a wide swath of humanity. I am acutely aware of the struggle of some older folks while crossing streets lugging groceries or parcels. I see the single moms toting a toddler, tugging the hand of a recalcitrant older kid, and I recall installing my kids on the bike and feeling free. On a commute from midtown to Harlem's 140th Street; I slog up Madison Avenue through the shopping mecca, past elite private schools and I navigate vertiginous hills until I zoom down past Mount Sinai Hospital wondering at the maladies that may afflict those waiting for a bus and thanking my lucky stars for a constitution and a will to bike. I continue on up to Harlem where the music flows out of springtime windows and the fruit seller seems joyful even on the worst days. I am inspired by what I see, how people make lives, find happiness and cope constantly to create family and community.

One year, on the Epiphany, I decided to begin a new sharing of the wealth I create by riding my bicycle. I can't share the energy, the giggles, the low blood pressure, but I can share the money I save. So I launched my Bike Fund.

Every day I am prepared to share whatever I save by biking. Yesterday, I went to the World Trade Center Health Clinic at Bellevue, two trips by subway and in fact it was a five-hour ordeal and so I might have sprung for a cab home. Okay, tally up at least five bucks. Then I went to a cocktail party and across town to a show. Let's call it another five bucks.

Now I have ten dollars in the Bike Fund. When I rode toward home, I spied a young woman with her sweet dog. They were sitting on cardboard with a sign which read, "Please help us." I wheeled around and gave a five dollar bill. A passerby chided me,

"How do you know she is not scamming you?"

"Well, even if she lives on the Upper East Side, this is a damn hard job, sitting on the ground in the bitter cold; and I want to help." He clucked at me and stormed off. I mounted my bike and continued home.

Later that night after a show at the New Museum, the chic crowd filled the Bowery smoking and parsing the performance art we had just witnessed. I heard one man accosting a group, "Hey, anyone have 25 cents? I am a quarter short of a million."

Oh, I loved that. "Hey, come here! I want to tip you over the top and put you on the road to the next million." I gave the man two bucks. This encounter made me think of a man I saw often when I went to visit my father who worked at NBC News. He was a jolly man who asked for a handout this way. "Anyone want to help me buy some Lawrence Welk? I love that champagne music shit." My father always contributed.

I rode to the Italian Cultural Institute on Park Avenue and 69th Street, a long, cold, bright ride in strong winter sunshine. It would have been so expensive if I had taken a cab even one-way, but I biked. On the way home there was a person who from afar was very androgynous. It was a figure in a mountain of clothes outside Marble Collegiate Church. I stopped my bike and popped it up the curb. Now, I could see it was a man, engrossed in counting change. He held a cardboard sign that read "HELP ME." When I approached he said, "Good afternoon Miss, how can I help you?" All intoned in good, smooth unaccented English, the clip to which newscasters aspire. "I thought I'd give you this." And I handed him a five dollar bill. "Thanks, have a good day." It was one of the most polite interactions I've had in ages.

I know with the situations crippling our world that my tiny Bike Fund is just a drop in the ocean, yet it allows me to help in a personal way. It always shakes me, reminding me how lucky my life is. I am grateful to have fallen in love with my bike so that I can share some of its benefits with others.

For the last three decades I have had the same sweet bike (knock on wood.) I know I can't count on keeping it and that the magic is not linked to the exact machine, rather it is the idea of biking which beguiles me. But last week in first spring exuberance I pedaled from my Harlem perch to the MET museum, six miles round trip. I was excited because it was my first big ride since tearing up my knee and I was determined to have a good experience. I propped my bike against a tree in the shade and went in to enjoy treasures from the Vatican and Hudson River painters. As I prepared to leave, visiting the loo, I had a flash. Had I locked my bike? I couldn't conjure the image of taking out my wad of keys and fiddling with the lock. I exited in a flurry of high dudgeon and prepared myself for the worst with a barrage of self-talk. "Well, you've had this bike a long time, maybe as folks are saying, you should get a newer, lighter one. Deep breath."

I approached and there she was alone in the shade. People rushing by, vendors with trinkets for sale and my old girl waiting. I was so happy. We zoomed home through a glorious Central Park in full spring opulence. The air was sweet, I felt lucky and enchanted. No public transportation could ever match that.

GOLD STARS

People who are well paid for their work don't seem to desire or chase after inappropriate (other) forms of payback—namely, the elusive emotional ones. Unlike mothers, teachers or non-profit toilers, workers in the well-paid field of capitalism receive hefty paychecks, stock options, 401Ks, vacations, all of which tend to alleviate the need for what I call Gold Stars.

Confession: I appropriated the term from my partner in a charity we launched. She is a shimmering young woman, ballet-dancer slim and whip smart but needy (Let's call her D). D just flipped over to 30. I am a chunky bulldozer of a middle-aged woman, and though I'd like to think I can equal D's vitality and appeal, let's face it, my hair is going silver and I'm more than twice her age. But we are both needy.

D came up with the concept of Gold Stars to illustrate our aching need to be noticed and appreciated. When we went on our last trip to Ghana, where our non-profit is centered, her sweetie filled a plastic sack with hundreds of stars, hand cut from gold foil. Every time I saw that clump of stars my soul ached. Oh, not a jealous ache, but rather a bittersweet feeling. That complicated hit-the-spot realization. I was happy for D that her man had given her the starry doses she deserves; also content to have someone else so clearly give voice to my long felt need to be appreciated.

Once, during my long-time abusive relationship with the father of my children, I queried my therapist, "How much attention is enough?" She replied, without a beat, "For an adult who was properly parented, any attention is enough." I wanted to inquire if she'd ever met such a person, but decided that this venue should be snark-free. I ponder that concept still.

I know I was emotionally undernourished in childhood and that I came to adulthood with a burning desire to be vitally needed, vocally appreciated and occasionally lavished with floral tributes. Instead, I am usually underpaid, scrambling for small fees, uninsured, under-supported for any semblance of retirement and often, in my mother's parlance, fishing for compliments. I suppose since I grew up emotionally wanting, I became a psychologically needy adult. So I was, and perhaps still am, willing to accept any offer. This augers that I am often poorly remunerated and feel underappreciated hence, fishing for compliments, or mining for gold stars.

Witness a few of my fishing expeditions:

"So... how was the dinner?"

You know, your favorite menu, the one I shopped for and prepped immediately after arriving from an 18-hour trip and then stood by the hot stove to cook for two hours.

"Oh yeah, it was fine, ma."

"Doesn't the house look good?"

After I spent nine hours alone mopping the floors, arranging flowers, folding the laundry, moving furniture, dusting and repainting it.

"Sure, baby, it always looks good."

"How do you like my hair?"

"Nice."

Really? I just cut 10 inches off the bottom and it's a completely different color.

Bigger issues abound and on almost all of them I crave notice, fulsome praise, thanks and wonder. A handful of those gold stars. But they seem to elude me.

Yesterday, I saw myself in another couples therapy scenario, still soul-searching, hoping for keys to quench my neediness and allow me to be more confident in my value and free from the constant desire to be praised. Therapy—whether it be individual, couples or family—often reminds me of an attempt to learn another language. Learning the skill of honestly sharing feelings, using "I" language – "I feel sad," rather than "you make me feel sad" – seems daunting. And even after years, I still have the sense that I am muddling through.

"How long have you been taking Esperanto and when did you become fluent? *Oh, about 30 years now and I feel I sometimes have control over the present tense. The past and conditional are still incomprehensible. But thanks for asking.*

So our therapist, in our bi-weekly session (which sometimes only convenes once a month), keyed in on me fifteen minutes into the session. She turns toward me and with that sweet smile she purrs, "So what you really want is for someone to come find you." Oh, don't you hate it when they suck all the air out of the room? And how is it that they always seem to target one person with the oxygen removal while the other half of the couple is sitting there breathing perfectly well?

But, ah yes, she was so right. I flashed to all those nights after fights, as I would wait for my sweetie to come to me. *Please, come find me, see if I am okay. Make it better.* It doesn't happen that way. The flowers are sent to others, the apologies made elsewhere, the dinners cooked or trinkets proffered by me. I wrongly think that mirroring good behavior will garner reciprocation. I try to do the right things, show how I would like to be treated. But after so many years, I am still the one approaching, wheedling and begging to be found.

I want to be needed, to be feted with a profusion of gold stars. But instead what occurs is that I continue to learn more about others. I know the buttons to push for my lovers, my children, my friends, my workmates; meanwhile, I am left floundering in a self-pitying, dark place. I think I ought to cut out a rafter of gold stars to illuminate myself so maybe others can find me more easily. I've done my part to find everybody else's sweet spot, now when are they going to come and find mine?

MIDLIFE MAMBO

"Even amid luxury, the ache of the unachieved seems intense enough."

Adam Gopnik

AUTUMN

HALFWAY THROUGH MY RIDE

I can't stop crying. I thought I was finished with the hormonal storms that preceded my period in youth and seemed to entwine me often in the final years of full-blown menopause. And yet, here I am, one moment content riding my bike against traffic, peddling to the gym on a foggy fall day, when without warning the waterworks start.

It's late autumn and the crumpled leaves – scarlet, pumpkin, eggplant and brown – cover the sidewalk and sneak into the street and the winds whip, stirring a frenzy. I am filled with emotion.

Maybe it's the shorter days, less light. Maybe it's not having small children on whom I can lavish attention for holidays, decorations and treats. Or maybe I feel all this sadness because I recognize my own personal autumn. Like the calendar, I notice that I have less of my season left than I have already consumed.

Strange to be sad about this, because in the calendar, Fall is my favorite season. It is when I was born. It encompasses going back to school, a place I was always so happy. It means cooler weather, even shorter days which I have encoded as longer nights, more time to snuggle and a better time to cook stews and bake goodies. Why can't my own middle age be this same joyful time?

When I am in a positive place, I can see that when my children grow up and move out on their own, it will be a fine thing. I am proud of their accomplishments. They are as different as day and night – my daughter loves social change, my son, the personal politics of sports. They are as diverse as their sea blue eyes from the tree brown; from her diminutive self to his stocky, muscular form. When I can envision them as safe, solid and fulfilled, I can breathe a little knowing I helped them set sail on their disparate voyages.

When I am in a dark place, I miss the baby children, the needy little ones, the giggling piles of squealing friends wearing costumes and begging for a half hour more of bedtime. I miss all the questions about the universe, the origins of god, sex or vocabulary. It is a wonderful moment, being a young mother to baby children. It is a time when you have all the answers and the questions are unending. But time marches.

Middle age is a lot like the ancient Roman god, Janus, whose job was the protection of doorways; he was also responsible for looking both backward and forward, assessing the past year and the one to come. Our month January was named for him because while tackling the first month of a new year and anticipating what is to come, we are simultaneously assessing the past year. Janus was a two-headed god, so he could face forward and backward simultaneously.

Now that I am in full middle age, I feel like Janus. I am consumed with constant head swinging. My mind jolts forward planning my future while I assess my past.

I can envision being halfway through my ride, life. It wasn't the kind of ride where it plodded up hill and then hit the crest and zoomed down. I see it more like a series of intricate twists and turns, with vertiginous, giggling highs and precipitous lows. Although I am sometimes sad about my less than vigorous muscles or my wrinkles and slower uptake speed, I still anticipate just as uncertain and wild a second half of my ride through life.

And in autumn, I have a man who loves me, and who really makes an effort to give me what I am whining will make me happier. He loved the round me I was when we married, and the even rounder me I am in middle age. He brings coffee in the morning and ends the night with kisses – the interstitial is immaterial.

On a macro level, I am terrified about my world and the world in which my children and my potential grand babies will live. I am frozen, heartsick and stomach churning from the outcome of the recent election. I can no longer watch or listen to the President of the United States; I scream from the other room if the news is on. I have lost my mind with that man, the role he crafted for us in world events and the fear they have so deftly sewn in all of us. I have assumed a mini-posture of personal uncertainty that is mirrored, unfortunately, by the world.

I find myself thinking at odd moments about how many more cars I will buy, if the refrigerator I have will be my final one (because I hate the shelf configuration), or if the scratchy sheets I bought on sale will wash soft in this next third of my life. Will I ever really make a difference in other people's lives or am I just taking up space worrying about minutiae? I don't ponder this stuff in a morbid way, although if my family knew, they would probably be horrified. How many more New Year's resolutions will I make, how many more semesters of school tuition, how many more dreaded mammograms?

Then there is a moment when you finally start thinking, "Hell, I want every single tough and tender moment the universe can toss my way." I have crashing realizations that every moment is rich and full of wonder when you are on a certain side of the ride.

Somewhere along this life ride I woke up and began to notice the coincidences, the magical convergences, the Jungian serendipity, the conjoined moments. I began to adore the process more than the result. There's no guarantee how much ride is left, so it's about time for all of us to hold up our hands and cheer when the wind hits our cheeks as the ride whips us around the next curve.

CAR SEX

It has been a long time since men whistled at me, ogled me, gave me a thumbs-up and called out lustily as I passed by. Funny, but sometimes I miss the sexism I fought so hard against in my early years.

I am fifty-five. I had the day when I melted men, but now I am in a different geological period; I am less volcanic eruption and more underwater activity. I love the wisdom, I cherish the friends, my kids, and the diminution of financial terror and yes, I even love being monogamous, eschewing inappropriate lust. I am not a fan of cosmetic surgery. I like my food hearty and my beauty routines minimal.

I try to find the silver lining in my silver roots, so there are times when I exploit my older, less sexy self. It allows me to flirt egregiously with young men, shopkeepers, cops, and the hapless tourists seeking directions. I couldn't possibly be hitting on them – I am safe, I am middle-aged.

I do miss the exchange of energy that comes from being noticed. Many women at middle age experience a sadness emanating from a palpable sense that we no longer turn heads. In fact, much has been written about the invisibility of women in midlife. But last week, I once more felt the jolt of energy that comes from being a head-turning vixen. I am loath to share how because I feel I should jealously guard the experience. In fact, my secret is nothing new; men have been enhancing their sexuality with it for years.

My desirability was pumped up to superhuman levels

by a car. This was no ordinary car; it was a perfect, 1964 silver, Shelby Cobra. I had the privilege of driving it around Manhattan on the last perfect day of autumn, ragtop down, roaring through the gears as part of a story I was assigned on a new organization called The Classic Car Club. I decided to drive the Shelby because it is my 17-year-old son Henry's favorite car. I was going to drive it and surprise him by meeting him after school. I knew it would blow his mind and, of course, raise his cool quotient.

Let me just say I am a woman who can drive. I double clutch, perform seamless downshifts, can spin a car, stop on a dime and know how to make a vehicle purr, roar, or in Austin Power's parlance, "Beeeeeeeeehave!" I am the driving product of a father who owned many sports cars and drank too much. He taught me to drive on a red Volvo P1800, then a Triumph Spitfire, and a British Racing Green Sunbeam. I drove well because he taught me hard.

On one of our first forays, my father took me to a steep incline, pulled up the emergency brake on the Volvo, exited, slamming the car door and said, "I'll meet you at the top of the hill." The car rolled, stalled and finally I made it to the top by waiting until another car pulled behind me so I could cheat by settling onto its bumper until I got the clutch and gas to engage. I was twelve. To this day, I can slip a clutch so that the car remains motionless even atop a San Francisco hill.

In college, I met the first love of my life. He raced classic British cars and together we renovated and drove an Austin-Healey 3000, the fabulous Jaguar XKE, and the original Mini-Cooper with its 10-inch wheels and 140 miles per hour engine. I love cars that are difficult to drive, I love the smell, the feel of the responsive wooden steering wheel, and yes, I love how people snap their heads to stare at me while I drive sleek machines, traditionally the bastion of men.

I was brimming with pride when the director of the

club said, "Let me show you how to drive the Shelby before you take off; it's a little tricky." And I responded, "Well, it's a classic H shift, high catch clutch, and overdrive five up and right, correct?" I aced the first shift, pulled out into traffic and the young director said, "Well, I don't need to show you anything. Have fun." And I roared off.

I headed uptown and heads were turning. Cars pulled next to me and beeped their horns. Young stockbrokers out for a smoke gave me the thumbs up, people cheered and smiled, and I could imagine they were leering at me, waving at me, loving me, appreciating me. After all it was *me* cocooned in the bucket seat, clutching the walnut wheel, and putting the car through her paces, exhaust pipes smoking. It was me downshifting and making that engine scream as I went from fourth, through third to second gear in a heartbeat rounding Sixth Avenue, leaving rubber.

In fact, I even received an email from my building manager inquiring, "Was that you I saw in the Shelby Cobra racing past the hospital?" Oh yeah, it was me, and I have never looked better, felt better, been hotter.

I pulled up to Henry's funky public high school on 22nd Street, and he was waiting outside with his friends. An unruly mass of teenagers turned en masse to witness my arrival. Henry strode to the car, tossed in his backpack, hopped over the low car door and settled in. He strapped on the racing seat belt and we took off, both of us in a different heaven.

I was super-sexy again; it was all about me and my power, my unique brand of gumption and panache. This was not just a fast car, a vintage car, an expensive car, it was a difficult car, one that had to be driven expertly or it would leave you right there. The car shimmied on the rough pavement, and then it exploded in a gush of power when I steered onto the West Side Highway as my son gripped the dash. I let her out, I pulled her back down, I revved past 4000 RPMs and then popped into fifth gear as the sun glinted on the East River and the sailing ships bobbed, and we hit 85 zooming into the tunnel. I downshifted and the tunnel echoed our power. "Wow, ma, that was great!"

Henry hardly knew the half of it. It was fantastic to feel this way again. I understand now why men purchase boy toys after a certain age. For one afternoon, I had a magic carpet that invigorated me past all imaginings and I loved it.

CRISIS OF CONFIDENCE

We have all noticed the phenomenon of people, mostly managers, being promoted until they reach their level of incompetence. We all know bosses, friends or co-workers who would work more productively at a lower level and, in fact, there was even a book called *The Peter Principle* that detailed this. I feel have reached the Peter Principal of middle age.

I assumed as I reached a certain age I would have accumulated knowledge, acumen, and skill; then at some point in my life I would be able to rely on my considerable skills to float along. I might have day-dreamed of being at the top of my chosen field, admired and mentoring many. But instead I changed paths and became a writer at 47. And to further exacerbate a dicey situation—in the last two years, as if I was in some sort of midlife quest, I have begun to take up a panoply of new pastimes.

I began playing the cello. I never played an instrument before. I never read music and yet here I am picking out Mozart on the bass clef. I am reading music, hovering over grace notes and attempting to find rhythm, pitch, and finesse.

I began an Italian class in the fall at my local community college and am now in the second semester struggling with the vagaries of the imperfect tense and justifying male and female nouns with their corresponding adjectives. Often it seems like a crazy Italian jigsaw puzzle and I can't imagine ever having the fluidity to find my words in the midst of the Piazza Navona. I learned French by ear very young and this is the first time I have attempted to learn a language by the rules.

I am also taking a pottery class. One of my daughter's friends has taken a leave of absence from college and I promised to spend time with her taking some artsy class. We settled on pottery and have been throwing pots for the last four months. I now have some wonderful misshapen bowls and idiosyncratic teacups with twisted handles in my cupboard. But I want more. I crave ceramic artistry. I want to be competent and centered with my clay. I desire the ability to make a beautiful shape rise on the wheel with ease while I gaze in awe at the mound transforming.

I am also learning to play poker. One of my Italian classmates is teaching me and I seem to be having a spate of beginner's luck. I have even changed my workouts from beating myself up in aerobics, with no results, to Pilates. This is a form of internal focus and slow, deep movement that has nothing to do with my natural proclivities to crash-and-burn workouts. Pilates seems to be restoring a modicum of waistline, so I must be doing something right.

I am struggling to find places where I feel competent. On the home front, my husband seems to still love me and I have a repertoire of successful recipes that I can whip up, and although not gourmet, put dinner on the table most nights. But I am the mother of two adolescents, and sometimes I feel I'm incompetent in that department. I certainly don't feel confident giving advice to my daughter who hates college or my son who behaves as if he hates me.

So all of this translates to an overriding sensation that there is no quadrant of my life where I can live in my own personal, confident, competent Sea of Tranquility. Even my normal solace of reading on the couch has been tainted because reading other people's work reminds me that I am having a crisis with my newfound métier. Reading non-fiction reminds me I can't recall half of what I read yesterday. In

Italian I can't hold on to the endings for the future, or in poker I can't recall whether I say "check" or "call" if I want to stay in, but not up the ante. I can find the most basic notes on my cello, but I have just moved up into a range of higher notes, written off the staff and quite frankly, these all look the same. So I am in a flurry of incompetence.

I have begun to revel in housework and my love life. Why? Because I can do a load of laundry, start a stew, pay a bill, or have an orgasm and feel competent. I can change sheets, store the woolens and take out the shorts, arrange flowers and have another orgasm. I feel as if I know what I am doing when I write grant proposals (my former métier), or make spreadsheets or cold call contributors to my local music school to garner donations. But that was my past life. What have I become? I am ravenous to learn new things, almost with an addict's passion, but at the same moment I seek calm competence. I launched myself into all these new hobbies and pastimes so that I would challenge my brain to build new furrows, so that my aging gray matter would exercise and get smarter. I wanted to develop some new skills in anticipation of old age. So I thought I should start at halfway there.

I envisioned myself playing the cello, speaking Italian, throwing pots, and even playing a rip-roaring game of poker with my grandchildren. I would be upright and strong from the core I am building with Pilates, and I would be writing whatever blockbuster came into my dodgy old head. What I hadn't envisioned was this middle place, where I was only marginally competent at just about everything as I construct my new skill set.

I suppose making any change requires being open to a feeling of incompetence. I listen to young children, hear them repeat words, phrases and point to everything, questioning, what and why. Seeing this innate quest to learn has given me the notion that being curious and inspired is a natural state for human beings. Maybe the luster dims as we get older because being unable to perform new tasks is unnerving.

So although today I feel as if there is no corner of my life where I am competent, valuable or even a minor asset, I will forge ahead in the hopes that as I fall asleep, the perfect set of imperfect Italian endings will waft across my relaxed brain and I will drift into a fabulous dream playing the cello, remembering well and loving my wrinkles wherever they appear.

DON'T YOU LEAK?

When my husband turned 50 I wanted to give him a spectacular gift. He had, after all, stuck by my side through scandal and teenagers. Sometimes the lines between these two events were very blurry. We began to grow old together, although I was leading by six years.

Zachary dedicated all his income to college, kids, homes and all the wild whatnots of life. He occasionally purred admiringly at a passing sports car, but not with prurient abandon. He learned to drive on an old MGB owned by his brother John who passed away years before we got together. Zach adored and revered John. His brother taught him to drive, turned him on to computers and was an anchor for the family. I vowed to honor this connection.

I began to look for a vintage MGB and found a 1976 model in great condition six months before Zac's 50th. I bought it; insured it and put on vanity plates that read "ZINC 50," in honor of his age and his company, Zachary Incorporated. I felt he wouldn't be anticipating any kind of fête this far in advance of a milestone and so I planned a big party in the country for Halloween weekend. I engaged friends and kids on the subterfuge and hid the car in our big old barn.

I am terrible at keeping secrets. The worst. I have been known to buy two and three sets of Christmas gifts because I cannot wait. And so my husband certainly did not expect me to pull off anything like this coup. At the party we all ate, drank and giggled. After dinner I asked, "Who wants to see the barn?" It was a newish property, so that didn't seem like a wild proposition. United, everyone crowed, "We do!"

And we traipsed up the long hill to where the barn light was lit and the new baby sat waiting.

I opened the barn and as Zac exclaimed "Oh my god" over and over, I worried that perhaps I had given my husband a heart attack for his 50th. He was over the moon with the actuality, the resonance with his brother, and the simple fact that I managed to keep my trap firmly clasped.

Thus began his love affair with The Baby Car. Old cars require lots of patience, tinkering and investing in the joy of the moment, because they will test your mettle by leaving you on the side of the road in a rainstorm or producing prodigious rattles that upend the calm of a country drive. But Zac persevered and stored the car in the barn when the first snow came, fought off the mice with traps and overly fragrant dryer sheets. Every spring right around his birthday at the end of March, The Baby would emerge and take to the serpentine roads of the Hudson Valley.

The spring the Baby approached 40, Zac hit 59 and I prepared to be 65. Zac took the car into the cement block garage around the corner run by an old codger, who for all the world is the spitting image of my father. Frank is so reminiscent of Bill Boyle that I often weep after hugging him and hearing him swear at me.

Zac told Frank that the car was mysteriously leaking fluids. Frank glowered his gimlet stare, rested his butt and badly bowed legs by perching on an upturned oil drum and said, "Hell, don't you leak?" I giggled.

But the older I get and the more I try to regain some of my giddy-up by taking aerobics, Pilates or yoga classes, the more I experience my own leaking and it freaks me out. I do not want to be a stinky old lady. I don't want to be leaky. I do my Kegel squeezes. Okay, not religiously, but I do them. I do sit ups, also not assiduously. For the record, I eat breakfast with the relish of a zealot, but everything else in my life is sporadic. Still, I occasionally finish a day like a troubled, wettish toddler.

I thought of what Frank the garage guru mused and instead of beating myself up for my aging pipes and hoses, I decided to look for a solution. I researched "pelvic floor rehabilitation." It sounded daunting and I certainly didn't want a steam cleaning or plastic surgery. What I wanted was to learn if there were things I could do better. There are.

First, I learned that many women who have had big babies do experience a kind of incontinence. Mine was diagnosed as the "latchkey" type. When I get close to the loo, or when my key is in the latch, that's when the drops begin. My physiotherapist told me I could change this, any of us can. First, she tested my Kegels. This involves an internal exam. Yup, I was doing them all wrong. Like most things in life, I think that if I overdo, then I am doing better. WRONG. So she got me to focus on the tiny muscles rather than using all the others: abs, butt and squinching up my face. Just a calm small motion. Not my forte. But little by little it began to work.

What is it that stops us from making simple, small concessions to age or personal differences? What stops us from seeking help rather than hanging our heads in shame and trudging forward, leaking all the way? With age, a knee injury, and some leaky valves I am learning to ask for help and follow advice. This is new to me and so I am also learning to go more slowly and have patience. I am perhaps more vintage or classic car than I care to admit. I am happier when I can meander and wind along, taking my own circuitous routes. And simultaneously, I am working to find ways to get my personal plumbing and knees more secure so I can venture out on more far-flung adventures.

REUNION

It is now two weeks until my 25th reunion from business school and I have decided to stop eating sugar. Although I have known this reunion was in the offing since spring, it has only just hit me. I have registered to attend and sugar gives me black circles under my eyes. You might postulate that in fact I have been aware of this reunion for 25 years, and yet, it is only now that I am focusing on it.

When I graduated, as one of the most unusual candidates from the nearly embryonic Yale School of Management, I knew I would attend one or two reunions. Even though I often felt uncomfortable and misplaced in that bastion of wisdom among math mavens and organizational charters, there were still folks and sweet situations I might want to relive.

However, when the time rolled around two and a half decades later I hadn't counted on feeling like such a slacker low-life. I suppose if I paid more attention in Quant class, I might have used my MBA predictive skills to look into the future. So now when emails pop into my box announcing an endowment of 150,000 dollars from a cranky classmate, I am shocked and wonder if my 50 bucks will be announced with equal fanfare.

When you graduate from a class that prepares captains of industry, movie moguls, and high achievers from all sectors, it's hard not to feel belittled by a lack of achievement. I have not opened a day care center for chronically ill children, or the first bank for African Americans, or produced mega-movies or been appointed to the administration. I have lived a day at a time, had amazing kids, and changed careers with abandon. Still, it takes a good amount of gumption to show up under-employed, and still possessing a too raucous sense of humor.

The classmate who called to exhort me to attend was (and for all I know still is) a very thin, bleached blond Republican whose father worked in nuclear energy. At Yale, we had some spirited, and on my part, *mean*-spirited debates. Why had she been the one to call? Why would someone, to whom I had been less than lovely, take the time to ring me and tell me of her divorce, from another classmate no less, and offer that she wasn't feeling so great about her thin, rich blond life? Was this the message? Do all of us feel undone about aspects of our lives at this point in the reunion timeline? What we two classmates shared during our phone call was unabashed love, delight and pride in the accomplishments of our children.

Is it possible that all of us believe, in some dark, shrinking corner of our lives, we are failures? My caller blurted, "I never imagined I would be divorced!" As if this were Hawthorne's time and she had been embroidered with a scarlet letter – only now it's "D." We all inflate our missteps and ignore the good things we have done; and that continues to astound me.

As my mother lay dying she asked me if I would answer any questions she posed. I agreed. How could I not? First she asked me if had slept with my high school art teacher. I had, but only after I came home from freshman year in college. She was giddy, "I always thought you two had such chemistry!" Then she segued to her life.

"Do you think my life was wasted?" Wow, now that's a conversation-stopper. And I was overjoyed I got to answer it after having my children, after weathering my own dramatic scandal and rebirth, and after having dialed back my vitriol from the initial onslaught of feminism. I am happy I had the presence of mind to say, "I do not presume to be the one who sits and judges anyone else. Second, given we don't know what the pitch and sway of the world is, suppose you were put on earth to have me, just so I could have Willi and Henry so that they might change the world."

Suppose and what if – isn't that what keeps us tuning in to the serial dramas of our lives? Don't you want to flip the page to see what tomorrow will bring? No, I mean really. I want to see it all. Maybe I am too omnivorous and perhaps my wide scope has kept me from making the big bucks and hitting the Forbes A-List, but it has kept me engaged, laughing, weeping, and thinking.

I know I am not the center of any universe with or without Pluto as a planet. So bring it on baby, bring on the suits, the success, the designer duds, the embossed business cards, the lush life, and the joy that I hope rained down upon these super competent achievers.

My joy is not diminished by my meager donation, by my comfy clothes; and certainly not by the mantle of love I tote around. So I am off to the reunion in two weeks. I know I don't have the time to cure cancer or rebuild New Orleans, so today I will finish this essay and I am starting to use the rejuvenating cream sitting in my cabinet for the last year, and no sugar! Well, right after I scarf down just one more piece of birthday cake.

ADDENDUM

I am back from New Haven and two days of classes on transitions to retirement, changing sectors, balancing our lives – all the buzzwords of a 25th reunion. I had raised my hand asking the weird non-profit questions, arguing for the underdog, and had been unable to divide my life into the neat pie charts provided. There was a section for volunteer work, transportation, leisure, family, salary work, fee work, and I raised my hand and said, "If I am riding my bike to work, transporting myself but exercising, thinking about a story I want to write and stopping to deliver something to the school where I volunteer, which section is happening?"

Finally one classmate had to say, "Well, you were always the outlier on the graph." The outlier is the furthest point that is still plotted on the graph along with the other points. That was and still is me.

He came up to me afterwards and said he thought I always asked the most interesting questions and they always made him think. He works as an oil executive at Exxon so I imagine my non-linear life, lived pursuing meaningful projects, would seem charming in some way.

I drove home feeling comfortable with who I am, joyful in my choices, but still firm in my commitment that during this next decade I'd like to make some money. I'd like to attend future reunions as the most outrageous member of my business school class, not the poorest. I hope my classmates will take their next decade to smell the roses, volunteer, and do some good. Turnabout is still fair play.

IN FULL VIEW : MENOPAUSE MAMBO

On an episode of a formerly hip cable soap "The L Word," where L stands for Love, Los Angeles and Lovely Lesbians, there is a moment when the very lush Pam Grier is on the verge of taking a much younger man for a lover. Yes, there is also heterosexual sex – this hour is crammed with assignations and naked bodies in all permutations and positions. So Pam Grier is attempting to talk this young suitor out of having an affair with her. She tells him she has been a thief, a heroin addict, a liar, a cheat, she has deserted her only son and all of this only makes her hotter to him. Then she drops the bomb – she is also in the throes of Menopause. "I am sweating and ranting, and in the midst of my very difficult change of life." Whew, this was a scene stopper for me and, I imagine, the entire hot-flashing portion of the audience. The young man is stopped cold and the scene changes.

Okay, to the producers' credit, in a future episode Pam Grier gets her man. Her suitor recovers from the initial cold water splashed on his ardor, but still it was chilling and funny to see that nothing could put off this man, nothing but the M Word.

As I sit, I can feel my stomach churning with a kind of heat-generating vengeance that will have me nauseous and beaded with a cold sweat. It is a sensation akin to a personal hurricane swirling in my core. After the swirl gains a foothold, it then radiates to my outer islands; that would be my legs, arms, and ears. I have strange heart palpitations and I feel dizzy, as if I cannot hold myself upright. I find the sensation, which I call "The Hotness" comes over me sometimes unannounced, but at other times, it follows my thinking obsessively about what I didn't do right or should do, or can't do, what I call negative thinking. However it comes, it unseats me.

The other day, our couple's therapist, a man, let fly with a judgmental remark. He noted that one of his other female patients, of a certain age, sweated like Louis Armstrong on stage. "Ahhh," I thought, "how lovely to live the life of a female where your bodily functions are on display at many stages of your life." Menstruation, pregnancy, and menopause; all our hormonal changes are public displays of womanhood.

You begin as a young woman with menstruation, a hormonal surge designed to get your body ready for childbirth and a stage that serves to move a girl into the realm of womanhood. Many of my friends got their periods, "their friends," or in my mother's parlance, "the curse," during school. They sat with that cursed friend in pools of blood, much to their chagrin and to the amusement of the boys. I don't remember my first, but I recall too many times when I finished a horse show or other sports event with a seat full of blood. I rarely knew when my period was coming as I had no cramps, and hadn't learned to heed the other warning signs.

Women learn to navigate life with our periods. Some of us take time off, retire with a hot water bottle or cool cloth, but in my house I was not allowed any special indulgence. My mother pushed for menstruation to be no different from any other time. She always knew when I was going to get the "curse." She said she could see it in my eyes. My mother taught me to ignore all sorts of pain. As I reflect, I see that sometimes she taught me too well. I ignored many of my body's and my spirit's indignations in favor of forward motion and putting on a positive face for the world.

In 1976, I ran the NYC Marathon as homage to my 26 years; a mile for every year. I performed this feat while I had both my period and an IUD. Crazy. I inserted many tampons in order to make it through the run without an accident. I even thought ahead to potential disaster, *The New York Times* had just run the very scary article on toxic shock. There was also a note, secreted, in my bra, instructing Emergency Medical providers to extract the tampons in case I passed out half way through. I finished fine, as I do most things, but with incredible exhaustion, bloody toes, and chafed breasts. I have always had a difficult time listening to my body, reading the signs and giving in to rest.

When women become pregnant it is more difficult to ignore the great upheaval in your body. It is not only you who notices the transitions; it seems as if you signed a contract with the world saying that while pregnant, you will no longer occupy your own body. Strangers will come up and touch your belly. They will offer prophecy about the gender of your child. Street savants prognosticate, telling you that you are carrying twin girls and it doesn't matter that courtesy of science, you know you have one very large baby boy. Even faced with science they will continue to discourse on the identical twin girls you harbor within your body. There is nothing you can do to stop this.

You could be in labor on the street and someone will tell you that you haven't dropped enough and the baby is another two weeks away. Or your nose hasn't spread, so you can't be carrying a boy. As you wait impatiently on line for the bathroom, no one will offer to move you to the head of the line, however many will come and touch your stomach. And this multitude will inquire after already depositing a meaty hand, "Can I touch? Is the baby moving?" as if you were the wife of the science guy and placed on earth for entertainment or edification.

Being pregnant means your body has been taken over by the Body Snatchers. Even if it's wonderful, you will still burp, fart, and even catnap in public. Everyone will see that you have been possessed. It is not like when you are drunk and you have the possibility of hiding your condition, or you have some sort of malady that allows a modicum of dignity while you convalesce or grieve: no, being pregnant is a societal condition that lasts for months. And it will prepare you for menopause.

As I waited in line to vote, two weeks overdue and huge with my first child, my lovely, unborn girl developed yet another case of hiccups. The midwives told me how some infants drink amniotic fluid and it gives them gastric upset in the form of hiccups. The flip side, said my ever-sunny midwife, is those womb-drinking infants nurse very well. As my girl burbled away, my entire midsection started jumping as if I was the star in a new alien movie. The line of voters parted allowing me to be the first one into the voting booth, but at that point what I most desired was my anonymity. I wanted to just wait patiently in line, unnoticed. But women in the throes of the various stages of what I call advanced femininity do not have that choice.

Take menopause: when I heard my therapist describe his hapless patient as Louis Armstrong I cringed. Isn't it enough that women have public displays of age in youth with menstrual mishaps, and then we carry the next generation through gestation accompanied by play-by-play action coverage, where each stage can be described by supermarket clerks, bosses, commuters, friends, and enemies alike? Why, after all this, can't we grow old with grace and anonymity?

I envisioned using denial to move through menopause. I would push myself through pain or exhaustion the way I did with my pregnancy or menstruation. What I hadn't counted on was the public displays and the shame I would feel at getting older.

Somehow I equated aging with something I must have

done wrong. If I had been more diligent, less lazy, more assiduous with my eating plans, my workouts, used more sunscreen, washed my hair more or less, I wouldn't be hexed with losing the self I had come to know. I wouldn't have lost the young me.

Sometimes it helps me to see my youth reflected in my children. When I notice tendencies that are similar in my young, vital kids it often alleviates the stigma. For instance, I have always had, just like my son, "uneven heat." From the time I was a tot I was hot one minute, and shivering the next. My son is much the same. As a big teenager, Henry still throws off the covers and screams out, "Too hot!" When he was little and the heat would come over him, he would roll up his pants legs, take off his shoes and socks and sigh, content as he watched a movie or a Broadway play. He created the comfort he needed. Why can't I feel that ease?

Henry didn't sense he was being watched; he was concerned with immediate comfort, not pleasing others or hiding from their negative judgments. I do not want to be noticed in transition. I am not overjoyed with aging and I wish I had more time in private to come to terms with my new self. I admit I relish some of the wisdom acquired, and wish I had heeded messages, signals, and signs more swiftly so that my early years could have been smoother and kinder. I am managing the gray hair, chubbier middle, sudden tears, even the wild dreams and interrupted sleep, but I do not want my body to be an out of control science experiment right in front of my therapist, my boss, my husband, kids, and friends. I want to have a sense of private dignity.

I understand there are a variety of hormonal replacements available, and on the advice of my wise midwife I did try something in the first throes of the change. Using hormone replacement therapy, I felt as if I was losing my mind. I am very conversant with craziness, but this wasn't a familiar idiosyncratic rhythm, it was scary. I have never been good at taking drugs and would always rather know at least it was my own wackiness rather than one induced by ameliorating drugs or even alcohol. So I refuse to take any hormone replacement drugs other than roots and herbs like the black cohosh native people have utilized for centuries. Still, I would like to have more control over when my body announces its hormonal heaving.

I have decided to create my own diversion: exercise. I have noticed that the hot flashes don't come over me when I am exercising. Perhaps they are scared off by the real intense heat created by my increased heart rate or maybe I don't notice the effects because I am already sweating. Moreover, I can use exercise as my cover. Having ridden my bike as a main means of transportation for decades, I now see that it provides a built-in excuse for the hot times. Most people know that I peddle my bike, uptown and down in winter, summer, spring and fall; so I say I just got here on my bike, or I have just been to the gym, or the cooking was so hot. I don't know what they think, but it helps me to feel somewhat private and protected and I love feeling warm biking even in northern winters.

I take lessons from my very hot-blooded son and always have layers so I can throw off or on, and I do so with abandon. Henry has a small fan right by his bed and switches it on if he is too hot. I switched sides with my husband to be near the window. I have always loved freeing my feet from the confines of the covers in the bed, and I now adjust from coolness or warmth: feet in, feet out. And when the churning hurricane swirls toward my center I ward it off with some deep yoga breaths, calming my entire spirit and restoring my regular rhythms. I then take the moment to see myself as healthy, whole and centered.

I see the "hotness" as just one symptom in a wide-reaching collection of changes that are happening to millions of women and me. I am not unwilling to move on with the program and step up to change, what unsettles me is doing it in public. I am almost ready to go away, chop off all my hair and let it come back in my father's shade of silver, maybe sweat in the privacy of a deserted beach or mountain – I could read books, ride bikes or horses and emerge, well, *changed*. In other times pregnant women were kept secluded until after the baby was born in a period called confinement. We all fought against that marching and petitioning for women to have full access to rights, jobs and the benefits of men. I believe we deserve them, but I would also like to regain some of the relaxed insouciance that I had about my life before it began to change, bubble, wrinkle, sweat, spread and gray right in front of everyone.

Menopause, like rainy weather, will not last forever. In the meantime I want some privacy, some dignity, some respect and a sense that my new self will be welcome whoever she is.

MID-LIFE HOARDAHOLIC

It is age or disposition? Do we realize, as we grow older that we are *hoardaholics*, keeping way too much or are we born that way and it only reaches a critical mass when we get to be middle-aged?

I notice now that I have kept far too much. I am holding on to too much weight, too many books, too much paper, too many old sheets, baby clothes, too tight clothes, sports equipment, and extra cooking accoutrements.

We are putting in a new floor in our front room and that means moving everything out. As I began to move our belongings out of the room, I began to experience an unsettling sense of clutter that went much further than physical stuff.

For quite a while I have wanted to feng shui my life, to simplify, to throw out and to have a breathable sense of calm surrounding me. What stops me? After all, throwing things away is free. I could simply make piles of books or toys and set them on the loading dock outside my loft. They would disappear in no time. It might even be construed as public service if I donate my business clothes, which are *way too small*, to an organization that bestows them on a needy, slimmer, working woman. If I gave away all the small baseball bats, skates and tennis racquets, some kids would be smacking and gliding in a park. If I gave away my deceased mother's capes some lovely older woman might be strutting her stuff happily swathed in a mohair wrap.

What keeps me keeping stuff?

I have to look at my body as the first indicator that I am not content to have enough. One does not become chubby, portly, round, zaftig or thick by wanting her fair share. No. Gaining and retaining weight and losing space in the house comes from wanting too much, abundance beyond what one person can use. Within that neediness is also a fear of needing something. That uncertainty then spins into the perception that one day we will not be able to provide for ourselves, or worse, for our family. And so we hoard.

Suppose when my college-age daughter gets her own apartment she needs sheets, pots, pans, mountains of books, or tiny ice skates. Suppose when she has kids she would like to have her own baby clothes. Suppose I need to be able to pull out all of John Cheever's novels on a winter night and begin reading without waiting at the library. Suppose some of these first editions are valuable. Could the child size spurs and velvet riding helmets ever be valuable by any whacked out stretch of the imagination? And who looks at the Samuelson's economics text from 1972? The Jean Paul Gaultier red wool coat from Paris in 1990 may be cool, but would I even consider putting it on, even if I could close it? Yet there they are: the fat old brown book and the glaring red coat.

When I answer that I can't see any use for this stuff cluttering my home and my body I still can't find my way to let go of it.

This supposition of potential value was a part of what kept me in a very bad relationship for over a decade. Suppose I let go of this horrible handsome man and he becomes valuable; I will have missed it. Suppose he learns to be kind, loving and employed. However, I released him and he continued to be unemployed and unresponsive as a parent. That was a remarkable lesson for me. I let him go. I made space in my life for a real relationship and subsequently found and married the love of my life. Why is it so much harder to throw out ice skates and sweaters?

I know that there are professionals who, for a fee, sweep into your house and douse the fires of clutter by ruthless culling. *Does it spark joy?* I know there are nutrition experts and body mavens who will do the same for your body. But I am a hardheaded individualist and believe that a woman must do this for herself. I have high standards and to many people my home looks quite neat, for a wide-open space with very few closets. But I am the one who knows what lurks under beds and behind bookcases. I know where my clutter is buried and it haunts me because I cannot find a way to release it.

The good news for me is that I have stopped the accretion. I know I have so little space on my bookshelves, so now there is an unspoken law: if new books come in, some have to go. I have even made some inroads in the last year. I have some open spaces in my home and I lost eight pounds leaving me feeling much stronger from my new workout regime. I'm accepting the truth that if I need something, I will find it, and further, I do not always have to possess everything anyone else wants at a moment's notice.

I might be onto something. In the meantime, I am off to clear the front room and cull more clutter. And work out. If you want some cool skates, spurs or books, check on my loading dock.

GETTING TO GRACE: CODA
ANGLE OF REPOSE

There is a lyrical, evocative phrase in engineering, a field not often associated with spiritualism; it is the Angle of Repose. Fixed at a restful 30 degrees, it defines the slope of a hill pitched so pebbles and dirt stop rolling. I have been searching for my personal angle of repose for a lifetime. I am on a spiritual quest for the place where my psychic debris comes to a rolling stop and peace ensues. And what I am finding is that with age I am moving toward that angle.

I have been on a life-long quest to awaken in a natural state of balance, into a life where I am full of grace based on the belief that although disaster strikes, it will pass like bad weather. It is an inherent hopefulness and resilience. Something akin to what you see when you watch a baby struggle upright and fall onto a padded bottom. We continue to rise and fall, again and again as we meander toward wisdom, and a state of grace.

I am a speedy woman; described in adolescence by my father as a broken tape recorder with only two speeds: fast forward and off. He further admonished me that my problem in life was thinking too much and compounding it by discussion. It was interesting advice, especially from a man who chose to quiet his own hyperactive brain with alcohol.

Every generation has choices and challenges. It seems that from Baby Boomers to Generation X and our children in between, we are on a pilgrimage to find spirituality or an inner life. Often we are thwarted in our quest because finding spirituality involves coming to terms with apparent contradictions in our lives.

I want to find calm, belief and a sense that I am not alone on my bicycle cruising the streets of the world. However, I am not a joiner. Pursuing organized spirituality has left me feeling dissatisfied, religions fit me poorly; like pants of an itchy fabric, a little too tight at the belly.

In sixth grade I thought I'd be a nun. By seventh grade, when a senior asked me to the prom, I'd jettisoned nuns for nooky. I explored running as a spiritual pursuit and finished one marathon. I sat through smoky ALANON meetings attempting to find the wisdom to differentiate between things I could change and those I had to leave alone. I tried meditating, but had trouble sitting still.

When the abusive union that produced my two divine children ended, I turned to yoga. I was skeptical because I knew I didn't want to wear a turban or chant unintelligible mantras. Hell, I'd worked in experimental theater, I sang and spun with the best of them. I wanted serenity. I wanted the obsessive thoughts to stop rolling around in my head. I wanted to discover true stillness. I wanted enlightenment, but I didn't want to eschew the occasional juicy steak, glass of Bordeaux, or the desire for orgasms measured on the Richter scale.

I walked the path of the Labyrinth at San Francisco's Grace Church Cathedral and revisited a basic tenet of my personality. In attempting to follow the complicated, serpentine path I gazed ahead, trying to anticipate the route to the center and fell off. Dr. Lauren Artress, the director of the Labyrinth project and author of *Walking a Sacred Path* affirms that many people have an epiphany in the labyrinth. "The walkers realize they are not human beings on a spiritual path, but spiritual beings on a human path." I realized that for all of my life I have been trying to look ahead to see what might trip me up and time after time I have fallen off the path.

I went to therapy to reveal secrets and tell stories. I wept through silk shirts and consumed a small forest of tissues. I eagerly looked for tools to unmask the joyful, hopeful woman who was full of forgiveness for herself and all those around her. The older I got the more I realized I had no more time for rancor.

I feel I am part of a gaggle of gals who may not have done it *all*, but have often done too much. I have tuned in, dropped out, been there then and am trying to be here now. All along I keep feeling there has to be something more. I have to be able to find just the right thing, add it to my list and make it happen. Instead I realized, after introspection: I had *it* all along.

The same lesson is told over and over in religion, cautionary tales, or popular culture. In *The Wizard of Oz*, Dorothy comes back from searching and exclaims, "If I ever go looking for my heart's desire I won't go looking any further than my own backyard, because if it isn't there, I really haven't lost it." A Buddhist koan proclaims, "When the student is ready, the teacher will appear." Even football, a little publicized spiritual endeavor, has wide receivers who proclaim endlessly, "I'm open!" I subscribe to a farrago of philosophies. I believe many of us do.

And now my spiritual pursuits continue with yoga, but I select my teachers to be those gurus who welcome the edges of society. I meditate, stretch, do Pilates and also attend a rigorous Hip Hop dance class. I kickbox once a week and need a nap to recover. I persevere with my wacky mix of "om'" and "grrrrrr."

When my daughter was starting puberty I found a Buddhism class for children. One of the requirements was that parents attend with their kids. It was in these classes that I began to notice my life differently. The most salient thing I gleaned in kids' class was the notion that all Buddha wanted

214

from himself and us was to be "Fully Awake." A laughable notion on the surface until I began to wake up more and more. I observed that answers might come to me when I was able to listen. I observed what many might call coincidence, serendipity, luck or the vibrations of the universe.

The calm seemed to come when I didn't worry, fuss or stress over life. For the record, I am not advocating letting go to the point where you sit on a tuffet waiting for the boss to call, your bank account to double, men to behave in politics or dinner to appear on the table. You have to take action and believe simultaneously.

For example I had a huge spat with my daughter when she was an 18 year old with raging hormones, about my anger, our anger. We retired unresolved and I rose the next morning and dragged myself to my favorite yoga class. The teacher dedicated the class to putting patience and joy into your life and your yoga practice. "Release anger at yourself and others and watch what comes back to you," she intoned.

This is standard yoga wisdom, but I needed to hear it that day and perhaps because of our fight, I was *able* to hear it. At times I want to complain that someone is making surreptitious phone calls from my house to the teacher, tattling on me. I think we all have these moments of coincidence when we are moved by the power of the universe, or whatever we call it, to toss some wisdom our way.

At other moments I want to chuck calm and belief. Like right now I am trying to edit this essay, it is 90 degrees, no air conditioning, the roofers have landed and are jack hammering in my head. I have agreed to house two French exchange students and somehow forty people are expected tonight for dinner. Who invited them on a school night? Oops, it was me. I start the oven, toss in a four chickens, and run away to yoga.

I go not because I am so damn holy, sacred or evolved,

but because for an hour I will contort my body as I listen to the drone of wisdom asking me not to judge, rather be present in this moment, and not in party plans, the story, or the dust settling on my floor from construction. And because my personal crises stem from doing too much, saying yes pathologically, and my secret belief that I am descended from a pack animal who is not content unless she is portaging a family of six across a raging river, yoga works for me. It allows me to continue to acknowledge my inconsistencies; wearing lingerie with sweatpants, enjoying finance and doggedly following my love of the arts, looking for calm while drinking too much coffee.

What's remarkable is that all of us have a personal angle of repose, and that is where we diverge from science and engineering. I see my friends finding different paths to that calm, especially in middle age.

Hallie, a stylist, writer and designer, follows the path of a Guru and still spends a bundle on designer clothes. Abigail is a staunch believer in the Christian Scientist teachings of Mary Baker Eddy and yet she took her kids for all their shots and exhorted them to do the same for her grandchildren. Carol at 82 has just published a book called "Yoga in the Morning, Martini at Night." Michael watches porn, but attends his alternative Christian church every Sunday. This is how my friends find their angle of repose.

All of these people are middle-aged and represent a salmagundi of colors and backgrounds and have all found a system of spirituality. They are not engaged in vapid spiritual dalliances, they are believers. At some point all took unspoken vows to hold fast to the notion that life would work, the sun would rise, but only sometimes shine. Life requires you to be ineluctably present; if you are, it promises that you will discover a personal congeries of belief to help slope your spiritual banks to the lovely angle of repose.

ABOUT THE AUTHOR

Wickham Boyle, known as Wicki, now a freelance journalist, began life as a tom boy, a feisty feminist member of her high school's all male soccer team and went on to be a stockbroker, a theater producer and was even once accused of being a jewel thief. She is also a wife and mother of two, and lived in TriBeCa from 1977 until 2016 when she decamped to upper Harlem.

She was formerly the executive director of La MaMa Theater, a world-renowned experimental theater in Lower Manhattan. With an M.B.A. from Yale University's School of Organization and Management, Wicki worked as a Wall Street stockbroker for 6 years and as an arbitrator for securities-related cases. She is a consultant to a bevy of nonprofits.

She has written numerous articles on parenting, the arts, and travel for:

The New York Times, MS, New York Magazine, The Downtown Express, Budget Travel, Savoy, Talk, and National Geographic Traveler. Boyle is the author of a book of essays written in the aftermath of the terrorist attacks on the World Trade Center, A Mother's Essays from Ground Zero, which raised funds for downtown schools forced to close during the crisis. Essays from Ground Zero provided a venue for Boyle's telegenic presence as a commentator with press coverage in The New York Times, Fox News and CBS News. In 2008 Wicki morphed her book into an opera which debuted at La MaMa and was entitled Calling: An Opera of Forgiveness. Boyle was New York Bureau Chief of Code magazine—and an associate editor of Grace magazine. Boyle was chosen as a finalist and invited to go on CBS' Survivor Thailand, but instead decided to accept an offer to write a documentary with Barbara Koppel on creativity. She further launched Thrive NYC, a lifestyle magazine for boomers and beyond.

Boyle's essays have been edited and recorded for the AARP radio program Prime Time. The first radio essay, Car Sex, was first aired January 16, 2007 and remains in play rotation. Everyone Won't Like You and Wisdom in Anger follow on a monthly basis.

ACKNOWLEDGEMNTS

Writing, compiling, and culling a life is the work of a dedicated, patient team. Writers writing about their messy lives require friends and family to buoy up their collapsing beliefs on a regular basis. It requires phone calls, retyping, editing, learning to navigate the new world of self publishing and a cattle prod to move a sluggish writer along in a world turned topsy-turvy after the 2016 election.

I am a lucky duck to have had the friendship of Nina, my college roommate, for 50 years. She has shown an unstinting ability to read anything and everything I have written since I was 18 and give feedback that made everything more vibrant. She read this. My great spiritual sister and former theater partner Annabelle took this work out of mothballs and sat me down on a regular basis and made me tell more stories, write them and then ordered them into what you read here. My "Bro Dave" who edited my book of September 11th essays has been a huge influence in sequencing and suggesting big changes. My smartest techie friend Susan is a grown up always willing to detangle the vagaries of the new world, and true to form she took on the self-publishing of this work. A new friend, Amelia, a PhD smarty in my daughter's circle, did the final careful edit.

Many friends as readers and supporters: Thalia, Kay T, Two Joes, Nick, Amanda, Marilyn, Hope, Sean, Kass, Handy Jack, Patti, Janet, Rachel, Abbie, Abby, and Abigail. And especially my wild family for cooking, listening and telling me I was crazy, annoying and wonderful in equal measure.

Made in the
USA
Middletown, DE